Decoding Logos
From Logo Design to Branding

Decoding Logos

From Logo Design to Branding

 HOAKI

Wang Shaoqiang

HOAKI

Hoaki Books, S.L.
C/ Ausiàs March, 128
08013 Barcelona, Spain
T. 0034 935 952 283
F. 0034 932 654 883
info@hoaki.com
www.hoaki.com
hoakibooks

Decoding Logos. From Logo Design to Branding

ISBN: 978-84-19220-00-4

2022 Second edition (Logo Decode)

Editor: Wang Shaoqiang

Cover design and layout: spread. David Lorente, with the collaboration of Edu Vidiella

© 2022 Hoaki Books, S.L.
© 2022 Sandu Publishing Co. Ltd

All rights reserved. Total or partial reproduction of this book, its transmission in any form or by any means or procedure, whether electronic or mechanical, including photocopies, recordings or inclusion in a storage and recovery computer system, and the distribution of copies thereof through renting or public lending, are not permitted without the prior consent of the publisher.

DL: B 15507-2022

Printed in China

Contents

Preface by Edwin Tan   8

Works   10

Designers' Index   290

Acknowledgements   302

Preface

Edwin Tan, Creative Director at Bravo

About Bravo
www.bravo.rocks

Bravo is a creative studio that makes and shapes brands that matter. It develops concepts with more boldness than Arial Bold, does art direction with more artistry than Game of Thrones, and produces designs with more finesse than Anna Wintour's hair. Bravo's people love what they do.

Logos are becoming simpler and simpler, to the point where you might wonder just how much simpler they can get. Even in the work that we perform at Bravo, a subtle tweak to a logotype is starting to feel like too much design. Writing this preface forced me to sit down and properly think about why this is so.

We have entered an era in which there are adults who have never experienced life without the Internet. All the information that we need is readily available at our fingertips—literally. Everybody is so savvy and well informed about everything. And because of this, people are more cynical as well, as they have read about all the tricks that brands play to make you buy their inferior products. They know that every product image has been Photoshopped. I myself seek the wisdom of online reviews even for my smallest purchases, up to and including dental floss. And if the reviews are good, the logo and packaging design are no longer the basis for my purchase decision. Hard-selling tactics rarely work any more.

An elaborate logo feels like just that: hard selling. When a logo is too elaborate, it feels like a well-dressed, eloquent door-to-door salesman trying his best to sell me cleaning solution—no offence to the salesman. The product might work well, but it feels untrustworthy. An elaborate logo feels like a smokescreen that is trying to hide flaws. In a time when magazines flaunt unedited, un-Photoshopped images of celebrities on their covers and embrace imperfections, in a time when people want their food organic, and in a time when Auto-Tune vocals are laughed at, I guess we are sick and tired of being lied to all the time.

The appeal of a simple logo is that it feels more honest. Brands with simple logos feel like they have nothing to hide. What you see is what you get. People are forming their own opinions anyway, so why try to sway them with your logo design? Another reason why I think logos are becoming quieter and saying less is because of the existence of social media. Brands have more avenues to connect to their audience, so the logo has less work to do now.

So has the logo become less important?

Recent tragedies have reminded us of the enduring importance of symbolic iconography. The Eiffel Tower peace sign painted by Jean Jullien went viral on social media and became the symbol of unity for the tragedy that happened in Paris. What this symbol—raw in its execution and yet sophisticated in its concept—stands for is immediately understood by everybody. Change your Facebook profile picture to the symbol and you immediately become part of a bigger voice while spreading awareness at the same time.

As a designer, this example serves as a reminder of how powerful a logo can potentially be. However, the logo is only as strong as what the brand stands for. The Eiffel Tower peace sign means nothing during peaceful times. And no matter how well designed Turing Pharmaceuticals' logo is, it will never resonate with people. It is common knowledge that brands go beyond just the products they sell. People want to be sold the intangible as well as the tangible—they want emotions and stories. They want to stand for something.

Works

Interview   Toormix

Tell me a little about Toormix. How did it start? What do you do?
Toormix was born during our last year in college, where we met and realized we work well together. After college, we worked in several studios and later decided to officially launch our own. We started as a regular graphic design studio focused on graphic design and communication. Slowly we evolved towards branding, identity projects and digital consulting.

Is branding a big part of your activity?
Currently, branding and digital have an equal weight. We see them as inseparable. Both concepts must be part of any brand strategy. No matter what, the expression of any brand must allow for its adaptation to digital form. Therefore, at any moment in the brand creation process, its materialization in digital form must be taken into account. Brands are now adaptable, alive, in motion, and one needs to keep this in mind right at the very beginning of the brand's conceptualization.

What type of information do you usually gather from the client before starting a logo and branding project?
We consider the preliminary phase of gathering knowledge and project immersion very important. In addition to more rational research processes, we complete our information through several brand workshops where we examine and debate the values of the company and its positioning vis-à-vis the market. We analyze trends, references and other interesting materials as well. It's of utmost importance that our research is properly defined, along with the dynamics that will allow us to examine and better get to know the company, its goals and, ultimately, its challenges and opportunities.

Where do you find inspiration for your work in branding and logo design?
Inspiration is everywhere. We're the first ones to shy away from specialized blogs, magazines and other similar sources. Knowing what's going on in your sector is fine but enjoying culture, travel and keeping one's eyes wide open wherever one goes, these we consider vital.

Could you give me a couple of examples of the branding projects you feel most proud of?

We're especially proud of the Parc d'Atencions de la Vall d'Hebron project. This is a multidisciplinary project whose goal is to improve the lives of the people, families and medical team in the outpatient care area for childhood cancer. It's a team that enables the creation of an experience: starting with the name and continuing with the architectural layout of the spaces and the interior design. It was designed for functionality and the wellbeing of the people who have to share that space.

https://toormix.com/proyecto/fundacio-small

What are the most challenging and most rewarding parts of designing a brand?

The part we enjoy the most is during the knowledge phase. This is when we gather the most relevant information about the project and outline the strategy that will differentiate us throughout the brand story (creative brief). This allows us to direct the conceptualization phase, which is where, perhaps, we can demonstrate our full potential; where we come up with a relevant concept that not only allows us to synthesize an idea but also to materialize it in all its possible forms, allowing for a clear approach at all levels.

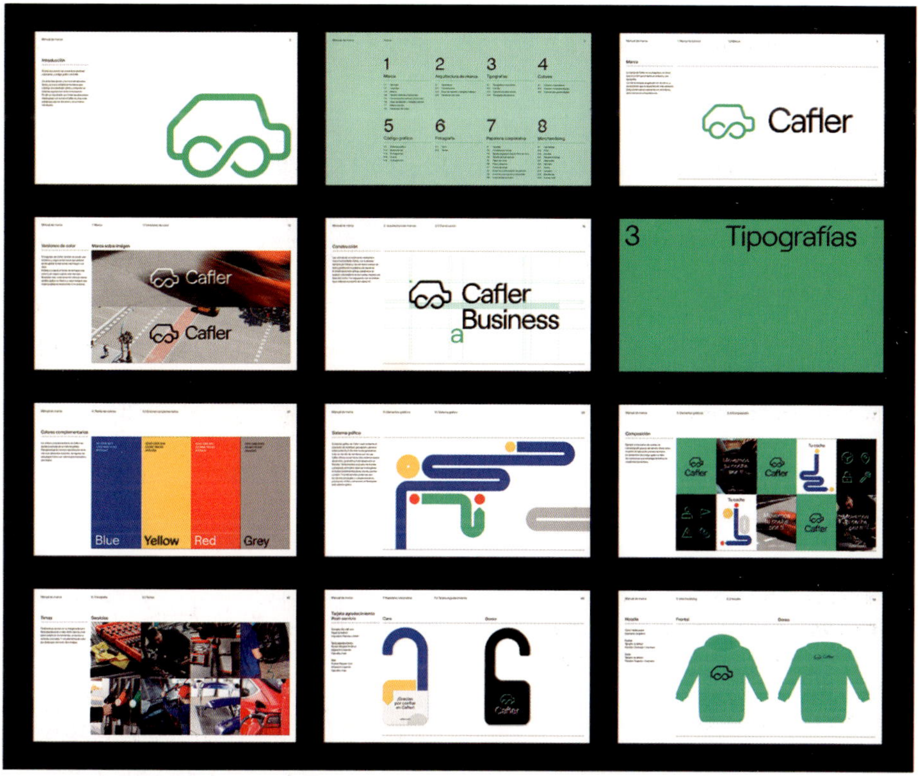

15

Mantra is the first raw vegan restaurant in Italy. It is not an integralist place, but a place where it's possible to test an alternative dining experience and a spiritual practice of well being.

Design **Supercake**
Client **Mantra**

Mantra Raw Vegan Restaurant

TASK
Rebrand for Mantra Raw Vegan Restaurant to express its distinct feature.

INSPIRATIONS & CONCEPTS
The architectural, graphic design, and communication standards for Mantra came out of the idea of a seed and of essence.

FINAL SOLUTION
Simplicity became the guiding principle for the whole project. It was pursued in the architectural and graphic design, their form and materials. The aim was to deprive everything of unnecessary frills and in pro of rigor, harmony, and functionality.

bīja
(seed)

growth

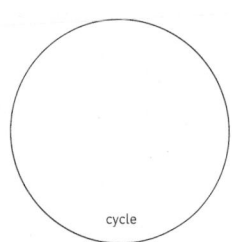
cycle

With more than 150 curtain lifts for around 60 performances throughout the 2014-2015 season, the Saint-Étienne Opera House is a landmark of great cultural importance and a predominant player in the cultural life of the city.

Design **Graphéine**
Creative direction **Mathias Rabiot**
Art direction **Mathias Rabiot, Adrienn Nagy**
Photography **Ghislain Mirat**
Client **Saint-Étienne Opera House**

New Branding of the Saint-Étienne Opera House

TASK
The objective laid out in this commission was to re-establish a sense of closeness with the people of Saint-Étienne through simple and down-to-earth communication. The main change was forgoing the "Opera-Theatre" name in favor of "Saint-Étienne Opera" to reflect an image of a traditional opera house for its aficionados, but also to draw in potential opera-goers.

INSPIRATIONS & FINAL SOLUTION
 The rooftop: An unmissable architectural feature, the roof of the building looks as if it is giving a sign. With its location from the heights of the Jardin des Plantes park, the sign looks over the city. For Saint Etienne's inhabitants it has become part of their landscape.
 The hall: Perfectly circular, the hall offers exceptional comfort and acoustics.

An accent on the top: On the top of the "E," the accent stresses the syllable by increasing the intensity of the voice. It decks the word "opéra" with the image of the building's pagoda. The opera with a capital "O:" The shape of the "O" brings to mind an open mouth singing an operatic aria. The "O" is used to show a strong emotion such as surprise, admiration, joy, etc.
 Rhythm is life: In opera, music and dance are intimately linked through "movement." This could be the movement of a body, of musical notes, or simply of the emotions triggered by these two art forms (the word "emotions" literally means "to make movement" of feelings). The emotion behind this logo comes from the optical framing trick between an "O" and the "accent." The "O" looks as if it's disappearing at the same time as the accent appears. That's opera's magic!

2006

2012

2015

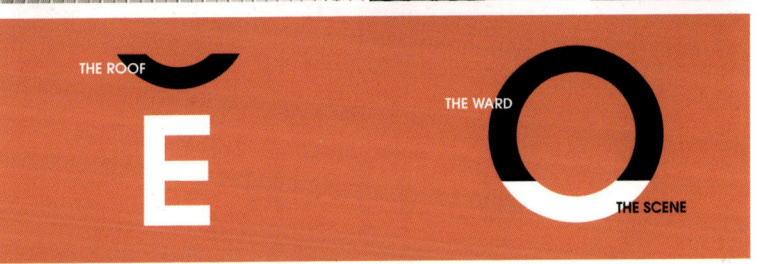

THE ROOF

THE WARD

THE SCENE

OPĔRA
SAINT-ÉTIENNE

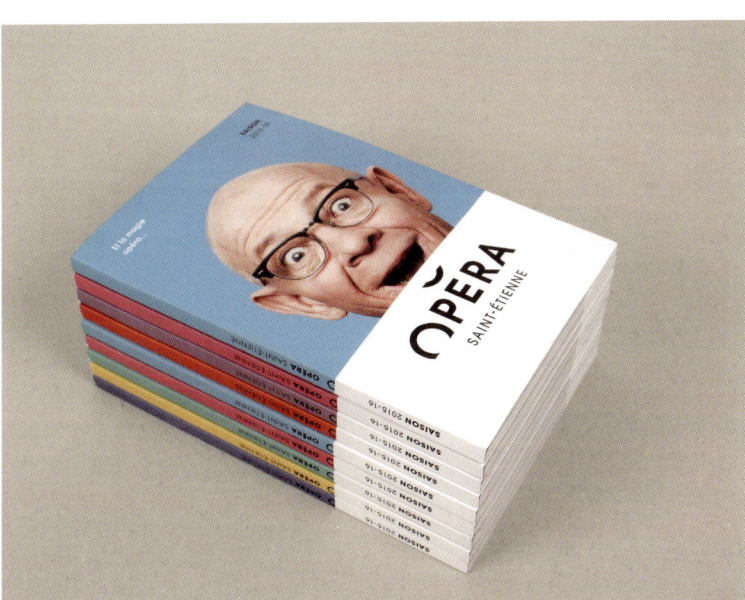

La Bottega is a highly conceptual version of traditional Italian cuisine by Chefs Paulo Airaudo and Francesco Gasbarro and a place for a unique experience of Italian food.

Design agency **Kidstudio**
Design **Marco Innocenti, Luca Parenti, Giorgio Franceschini**
Client **La Bottega Italia**

La Bottega – Cucina Italiana

TASK
Branding project for a restaurant that will soon become a chain of restaurants, pizzerias, and traditional Italian trattorias.

INSPIRATIONS & CONCEPTS
The designer wants a feeling of simplicity, minimalism, and sobriety with an accent and shows the Italian food in his authentic face without the regular clichés.

FINAL SOLUTION
A logo in a custom bodonian typeface; colors and papers chosen to give a rough and earthly feeling.

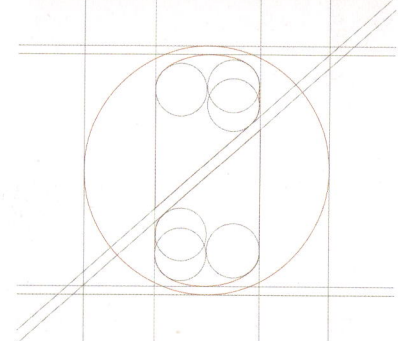

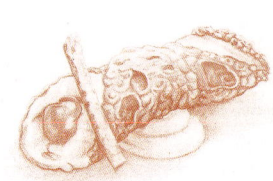

The Collection is a restaurant, a cultural event, and a retail space.

Design **Mind Design**
Client **The Collection**

The Collection

TASK
The team was assigned to design the identity, the signage system, and all printed materials.

INSPIRATIONS & CONCEPTS
The idea for the identity related to multiple prints, limited editions, and artist signatures. The execution was relatively simple: everything was based on an A5 format with punched holes.

FINAL SOLUTION
The team used screen printing which allowed them to change colors on the printing bed and make each print unique. Larger signs were made up by several A5 boards and the thickness was achieved by hanging several signs in front of each other. For the logo the team asked the client to write the name in their own handwriting connecting two dots equivalent to the punched holes.

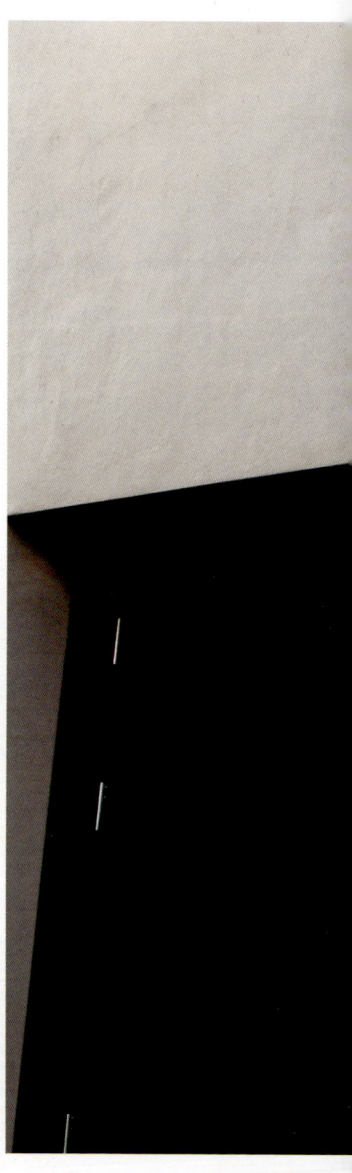

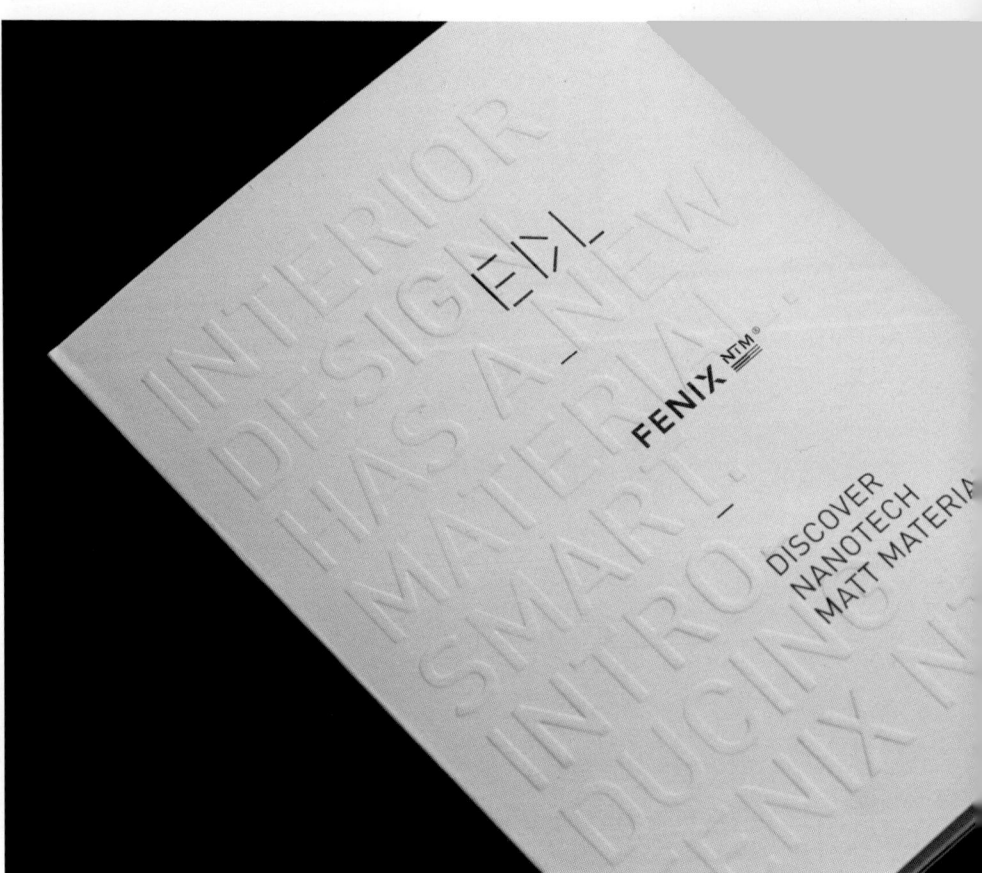

Frigolab San Mateo is a privately owned company located in Manta, Ecuador. It is a member of the Alfa Gamma Group, a conglomerate of seafood companies which operates seven fishing fleets in Ecuador, Panama, Peru, Suiname, Mexico, and the United States. San Mateo has been in business for more than 20 years, engaged in harvesting, processing, exporting, and marketing fresh and frozen ocean seafood.

Design **Freddy Agostini**
Creative direction **Cesar Sepulveda, Fabian Martinez**
Client **San Mateo**

San Mateo Frozen Seafood

TASK
The task was to develop a logo for its own frozen food products "San Mateo," a new product to be commercialized in supermarkets. The logo had to stand out from the rest of its competitors, and allow an easy recognition for its upper middle class customers.

INSPIRATIONS & CONCEPTS
There are many ways to create a visual identity for a brand. Among them, minimalism is a growing trend that favors simplicity and clarity over excessive ornamentation. Minimal designs put a brand and its message before form, allowing for better recognition and easier communication with their customers.

FINAL SOLUTION
During the design process, the team focused on achieving 2 key qualities: simplicity and legibility. They paid special attention to the design of a fresh and unique logo, conceptually using the "S" of "San Mateo" as a hook, and its negative space as a fish shape which promised new discoveries, achievements, harmony, and unity.

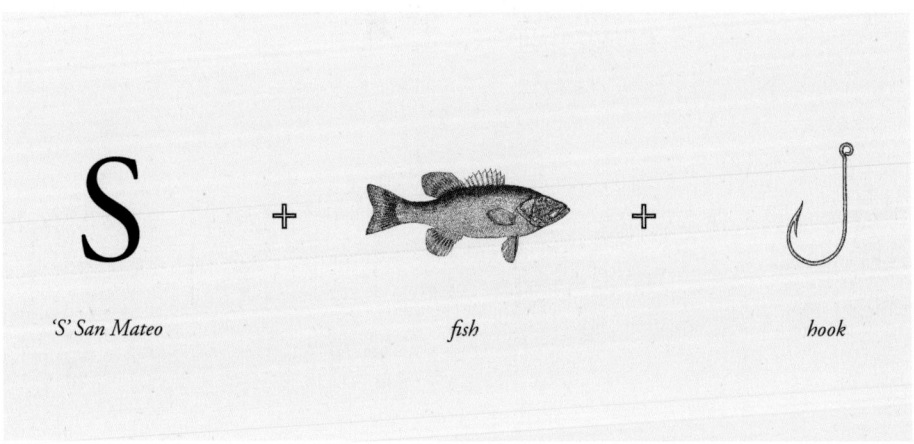

'S' San Mateo   fish   hook

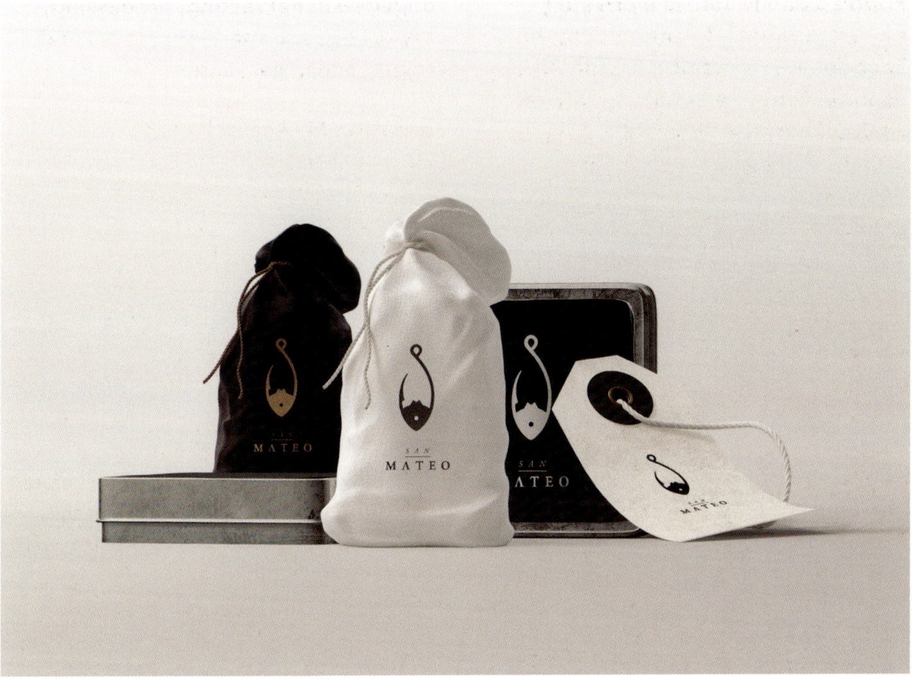
SAN
MATEO
SAN
MATEO

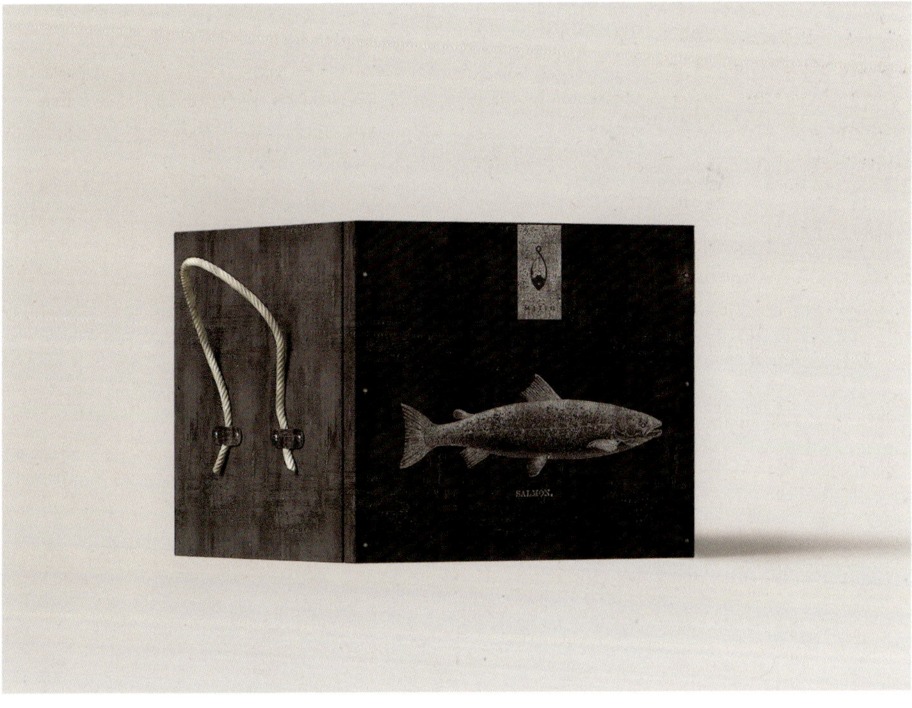
SALMON.

Runster is a website addressing to people whose primary exercise is running or to those who think of starting running as a hobby. The site gives notice, ideas, solutions, and instructions to prospective runners in order to inform and innovate in the issue of "running."

Design agency **Cloudtrap Design Studio**
Creative direction **Fedon Arvanitakis**
Client **Runster gr**

Runster

TASK
The client trusted the studio, in order for his online company to acquire a complete identity. The team began from his brief and continued with research on running, lifestyle, men and women runners, and their accessories. The goal was to create a well-defined, distinctive, and highly aesthetic logo which would perfectly connect with Runster's philosophy.

INSPIRATIONS & CONCEPTS
The team found many "key words" through a survey including the "city" (all people who exercise by running, do it mostly in the cities where they live); the "itinerary" (each runner selects a route, either short or long, always setting however the starting and finishing point); the "digital era" (it could not be missing, since the whole world involves around the web and Runster, and the brand is a "digital" media firm); the "lion" (the team searched in nature for the authentic "Runster"); the "R" (in their solution, they decided all of the above to be linked with the initial letter of "Runster").

FINAL SOLUTION
Their final solution basically consists of the keywords which they visualized in a quite particular style. The logo joins all these ideas and becomes one. The city, the itinerary, the digital era, and the lion become one and form the letter "R." The lion is looking back because he is the pioneer and the only one who controls what happens behind him. The use of only one color marks the brand, and also facilitates its different applications, since the sector of running already includes a lot of color. The font (San Francisco Text) remains simple, clean but "heavy" and constant, as every Runster's steps should be, illustrating at the same time the consistency of the brand.

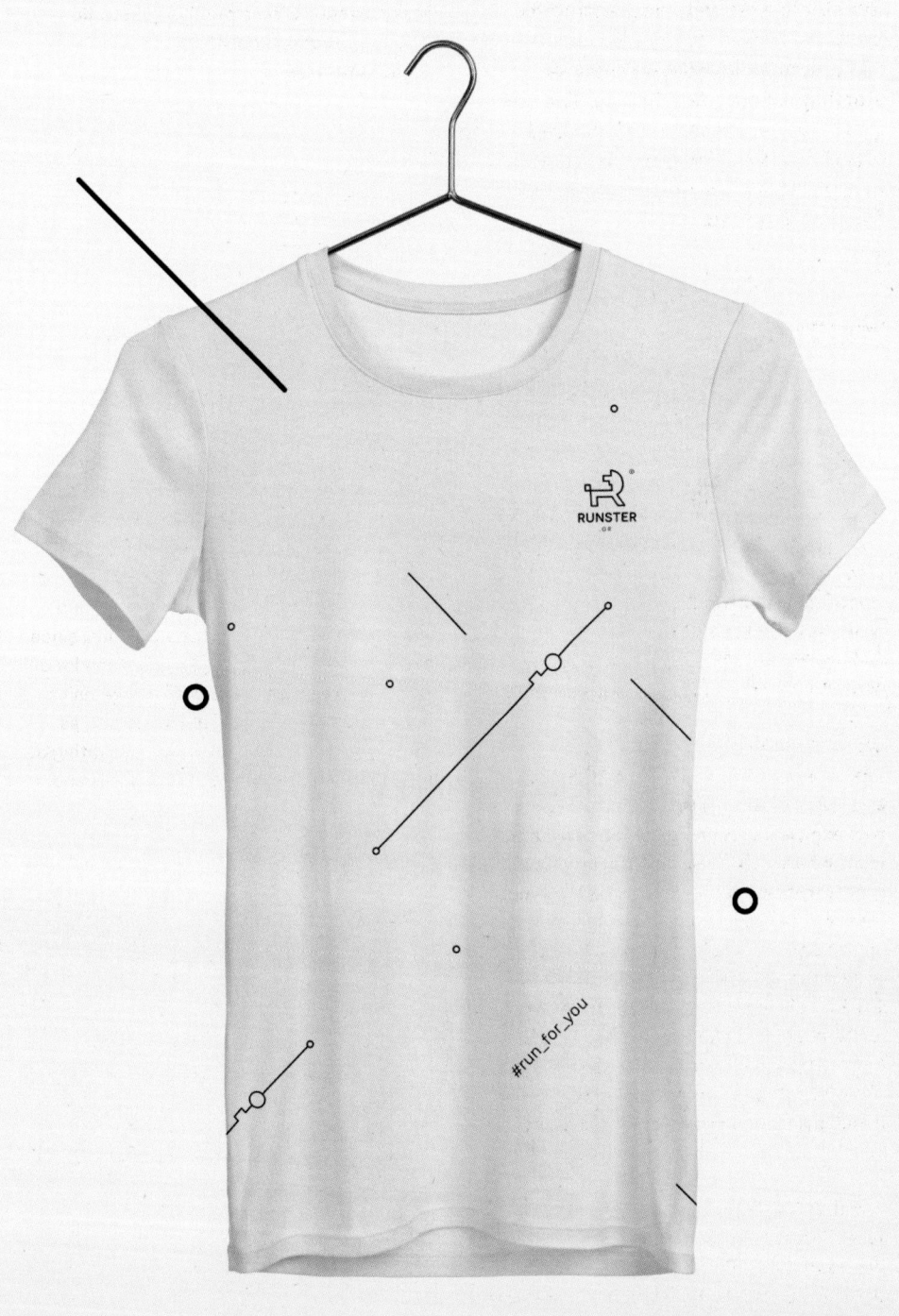

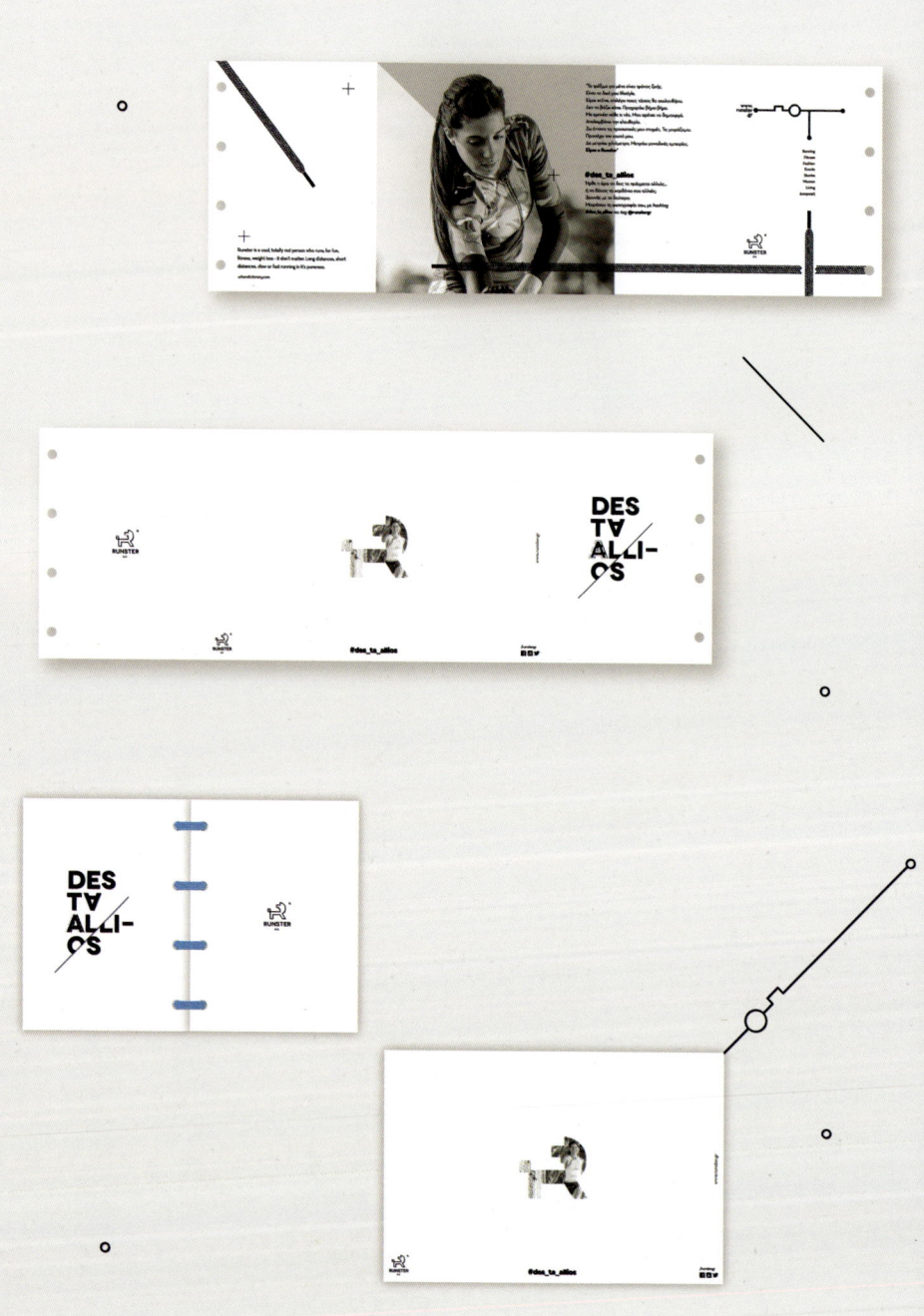

Troglodytes Music is the brand name of Giuliano Forghieri, scores preparation and elaboration for publishing houses and musicians in search of top class quality.

Design **Jorge Castano**
Client **Pomodoro Web Agency, Giuliano Forghieri**

Troglodytes Music Branding

TASK
Create a brand identity that represents the passion of Giuliano Forghieri: the troglodytes bird and the music, a brand that represents a high standard of music and design.

INSPIRATIONS & CONCEPTS
The main inspiration was the troglodyte bird and the music. Together they give the concept of versatility, harmony, and freedom of the music.

FINAL SOLUTION
The final solution was the mix of troglodyte bird and the G-clef, making a single object that represents all the values that the musician wanted to give to his brand.

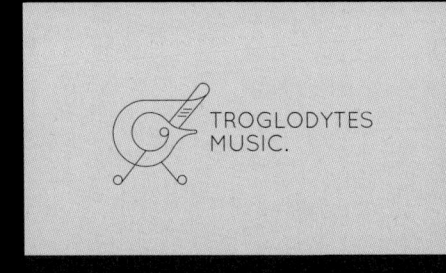

Eclectic is a restaurant in Paris located in the 15th arrondissement, quartier Beaugrenelle, an area characterized by a diverse mix of architecture and brutalist concrete buildings from the '60s.

Design **Mind Design**
Client **Eclectic**

Eclectic

TASK
Mind Design was assigned to design the overall identity for Eclectic.

INSPIRATIONS & CONCEPTS
The identity concept is based on two contrasting visual concepts that were prominent in the '60s: the geometric and the fluid, the hard and the soft.

FINAL SOLUTION
Accordingly the design features a rigid grid of straight lines whereby occasionally those lines change into random fluid shapes.

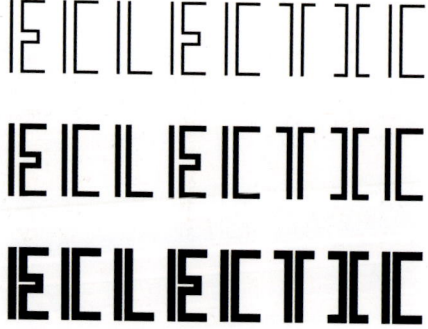

45

J'EDITORIA is a select shop based in Taipei. The shop owner Jane has selected different products from apparels to accessories through travel and life experiences, which are mainly from Europe and America. Hence Taiwanese customers are able to purchase these fashion brands easily.

Design agency **Transform Design**
Design **Yueh Hsin Yi**
Art direction **Huang Kuo Yu**
Client **J'EDITORIA**

J'EDITORIA

TASK
The target group of J'EDITORIA is mainly female. Therefore, the logo should approach to female market. In order to enhance the impression of customers, the team defines the brand personality of J'EDITORIA within this big market.

INSPIRATIONS & CONCEPTS
The concept needs to be clear and the logotype should look classic and elegant.

FINAL SOLUTION
EDITORIA means "publishing" in Italian. The symbol combines the initials of the shop owner's name "Jane" and "EDITORIA." Strength and grace merge to form a simple design. The minimal and cozy style represents the core personality of J'EDITORIA. In addition, the team used the logo to design different patterns for shopping bags which became helpful for brand promotion.

J'EDITORIA

Saint-Didier-au-Mont-d'Or is located on the ridges forming the southern foothills of the small Mont d'Or, next to the 9th district of the city of Lyon. This geographical position gives it a unique living environment close to the major economic centers of Vaise or Écully. It is therefore an area between town and country.

Design **Graphéine**
Creative direction **Mathias Rabiot**
Art direction **Mathias Rabiot, Adrienn Nagy**
Client **City of Saint-Didier-au-Mont-d'Or**

New Branding of the Saint-Didier-au-Mont-d'Or

TASK
The task was to rebrand the city of Saint-Didier-Au-Mont-d'Or.

INSPIRATIONS & FINAL SOLUTION
The name "Saint-Didier-au-Mont-d'Or" is particularly long. Its uniqueness lies in the fact that these five words are linked together by four hyphens.

The symbol of the hyphen is the "encounter" between different sections of the same object, which generates meaning: preserving vital link between all the people, all generations, associative dynamics, and the municipal team. Making this typographical sign as the identity element of the city is a promise of creating links, links between city and countryside, people, generations, etc.

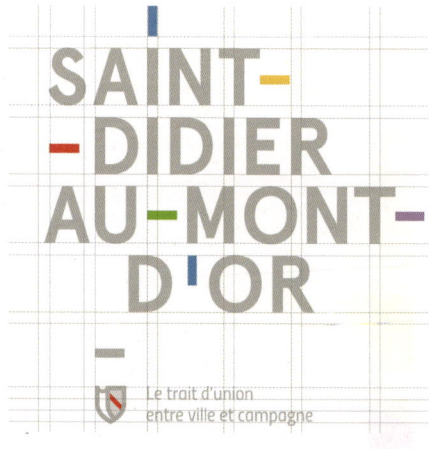

50

51

EDL

TASK
To mark their tenth anniversary and expansion onto an international stage, the company embarked on a rebrand to propel them in their journey forward.

INSPIRATIONS & CONCEPTS
The bold strokes that form the logo were inspired by the visual metaphors found everywhere in nature, crisp in shape, yet versatile in structure. Guided by EDL's philosophy to inspire experiences, each brand collateral was designed to inspire and excite. The team paid close attention to tactile finishings, patterns, and carefully chosen visuals to communicate this philosophy.

FINAL SOLUTION
The team set out to create a new identity that embodied EDL's state of mind– one that was decluttering and always reinventing. Like basic building blocks, the EDL logo was an amenable tool that could take on multiple personalities integrating effortlessly into every story.

New Logotype

At half the weight point of main logotype.

New Seal Logo

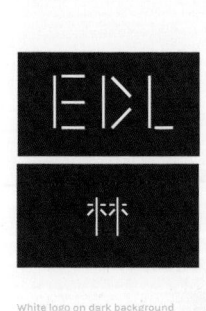

White logo on dark background

53

A "mercadito" is a popular market traditionally meant to trade basic goods, while Mercadito de Arte gallery is trading arts in the same way. Mercadito de Arte thinks of art as a basic need, so it shouldn't be just for a few any more than education should not be just for a few either. The gallery is looking to bridge the public's increasing interest in art with scenes of contemporary and relatively unknown artists, especially those not carrying a premium for reputation.

Design **Apofenia**
Client **Mercadito de Arte**

Mercadito de Arte

TASK
The client already had a name for the gallery, so the team was consulted regarding the development for the brand. They were asked to develop the communication strategy, logotype, and visual identity, and to propose a kit of branded stationery for the daily business duties.

INSPIRATIONS & CONCEPTS
The concept the team chose for the brand was called "Affordable Art for the People," so their identity proposal was inspired by the crossover between traditional popular markets and the museographic style of contemporary galleries. This led the team to design a sophisticated wordmark along with a line of peripherals on grays and a slight accent of color.

FINAL SOLUTION
The logo consists of only letters and lines, all set in Tobias Frere-Jones' Gotham Bold. A vertical and a horizontal version were prepared to better suit any given format. The colors for the logo are only black and white; for other branded elements gray and pink were used, inspired by the color of concrete and the metallic tubes seen on traditional markets. The result was a functional and straightforward communication of the brand's objectives.

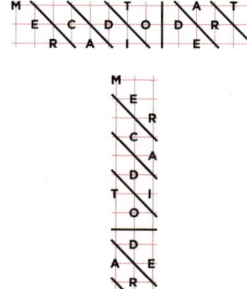

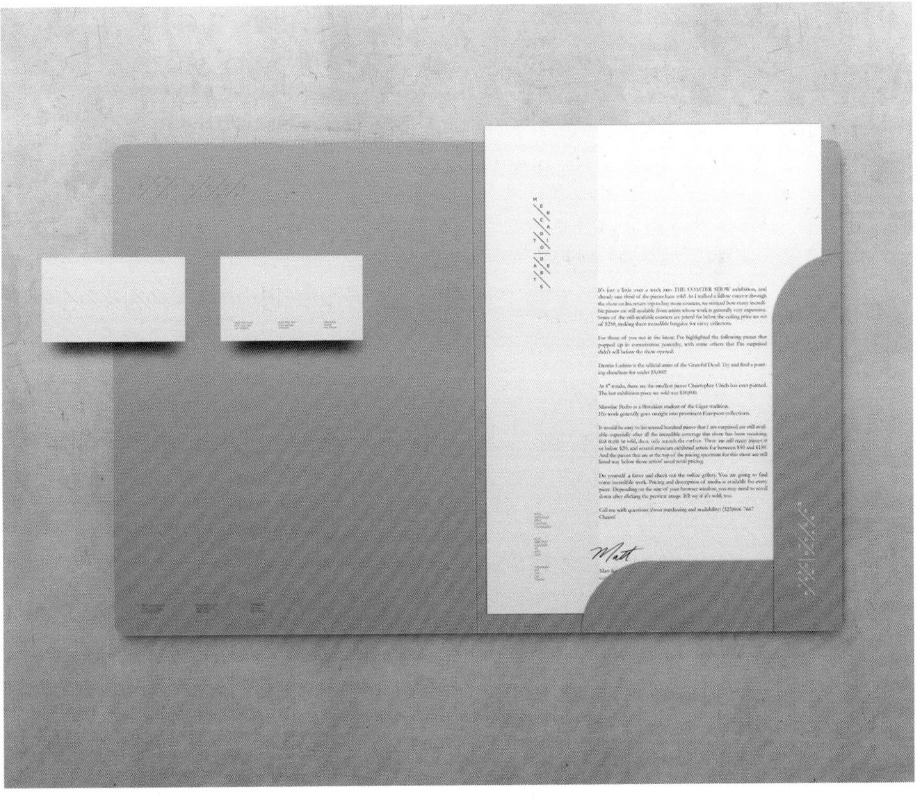

The Fontevraud Abbey is a former Benedictine monastery, seat of the Order of Fontevraud, founded in 1101 by Robert d'Arbrissel and located in Fontevraud, near Saumur, France. It is one of the largest monastic cities in Europe. The French Revolution bears a definitive stop to the religious establishment and transforms the abbey into a prison until 1963. The various buildings renovations have begun in the 19th century after the classification of the abbey as historical monuments and continues to this day. In 2000, Fontevraud Abbey is declared as a World Heritage Site by UNESCO with the entire cultural landscape of the Loire Valley.

Fontevraud – Branding

TASK
The project of creating the brand Fontevraud shows exceptional political and economic will, and a great desire for modernity and excellence. It expresses the ambition of a program to be visible and understandable across the venue as much as outside its borders. It must be remarkable, but above all, value the territory. The Abbey of Fontevraud is a historical monument that belongs to our heritage. It needs to be preserved, protected, and restored. We are facing here strong signs that can be intimidating by their history and architectural qualities.

INSPIRATIONS & FINAL SOLUTION
The conceptual starting point is the permeability between the notions of sacred and profane. Indeed, it is worth recalling that if Fontevraud was a Royal Abbey for over 6 centuries, Napoleon saved the abbey from demolition by turning it into a prison. In 1975, the Royal Abbey opened to the public, thus putting an end to 9 centuries' behind closed doors. Thus, from this long history, the team chose to focus their attention on this antinomy: Sacred/Profane.

The team chose to symbolize the sacred with the variation of a graphic element named the "HALO." Profane is represented by a typographical writing that draws his spelling of "SLASH". The articulation between "HALO" and writing "SLASH" is the basis of the visual identity of Fontevraud.

Design **Graphéine**
Creative direction **Jérémie Fesson,
Mathias Rabiot**
Art direction **Sophie Rueter, Philip De Canaga**
Client **Abbaye Royale de Fontevraud**

Interview   Graphéine

Tell me a little about Graphéine. How did it start? What do you do?
Graphéine started in 2002, right after completing our studies, when we started our own business in a small apartment.

For 10 years, we were 5 friends working together on all types of subjects (print, digital, signage...).

In 2012, a new period began. We are both passionate about visual identities. The agency specializes in visual identities. Our teams are always growing thanks to a wealth of talent. Today we are a team of about fifteen based in Lyon and Paris.

Is branding a big part of your activity?
The agency only works on subjects related to brand image. We help our clients define their positioning or communication issues, and then we design visual and sometimes verbal responses. In addition, we work with our clients on numerous applications that stem from our work on brand identity.

What type of information do you usually gather from the client before starting a logo and branding project?
There is no "typical" information to gather. Each client is unique. We take some time to explore the client's world. We learn about the challenges of their business, we analyze their market, we hear from their employees, we scrutinize data, we read reference books... and above all we ask our client questions. In short, we form an informed opinion in order to identify a problem.

Where do you find inspiration for your work in branding and logo design?
We have a strong general knowledge of logo design. We buy books, we follow the news, we attend conferences and we edit a blog to document and share the accumulated knowledge with our teams and the wider community.

Could you give me a couple of examples of the branding projects you feel most proud of?
We are proud of all our projects. It's not sycophancy.

We strive to ensure that every project that the agency takes on is something we can be proud of.

Sometimes it's the boldness of the creation; other times it's simply the collaboration with the client that was pleasing.

We like to help our clients progress. For example, designing a beautiful project with a cultural client is quite simple, while making an original logo for an industrial company is more complex. We like this complexity, even if the result will not necessarily be the most creative project. What matters is finding the "right" answer.

I sense a strong architectural component in some of your projects. Is this something you are aware of?
It's hard to be objective about one's own work. It's true that graphic design and architecture are sister disciplines. Both work with space. The architect conceives of the volume (3D), the graphic designer of the plan (2D). But the design processes are similar. We work with geometry, with fullness and emptiness, with shadow and light.

What are the most challenging and most rewarding parts of designing a brand?
Two aspects are exciting in this job.
The designer can be seen as a mediator who collaborates with numerous clients in multiple disciplines and with a plethora of partners. Our work is at the heart of the transformation processes of organizations, and we can draw on a wide range of disciplines, including science, technology, the arts, economics, sociology, anthropology and the environment, to carry out these projects. All of this contributes to our knowledge of others, offering us a broad vision of society and the issues of our time.

The other stimulating aspect of this job is to feel useful. Our signs are widely distributed in the public space. Coming across a logo on a street corner on which you have worked for 6 months, spent hours making optical corrections or fought to validate a certain color produces a very strong feeling of satisfaction. This emotional bond with our creations is a reflection of the passion involved. And even if the authorship of these creations is always collective, each of us finds in them a piece of his or her own unique intelligence and ability.

In the end, each of us feels symbolically part of our clients' worlds. This feeling is built little by little, through the sharing of realities, values and objectives.By helping to forge one's identity, it pushes one to give the best of oneself and contributes to feeling proud to be part of this world.

Olaqin

RAUM is a fictional brand for a multifunctional place where new things can be learnt, knowledge is shared, and mistakes can be made. It is a workspace for people who enjoy being creative, a space that can be used as an atelier but can be easily turned into a room for workshops, exhibitions, and parties. The website keeps the clients updated on the events that take place at RAUM and sells selected design items.

Design **Daniel Farò, Lisa-Marie Kaspar**
Client **RAUM**

RAUM

TASK
In the 3rd semester of their studies, Lisa-Marie and Daniel both had attended the course "Corporate Design" by Professor Carl Frech in which a fictional brand had to be invented and then an identity for it had to be made. The main focus was to create an identity that fitted the brand perfectly, based on consistent rules and structure.

INSPIRATION & CONCEPTS
The main reason for the team to create RAUM was that they loved the thought of a shared workspace for artists, creative persons, and those interested in art and design in general. The thought of creating and learning by working together with others was also very important. Inspirations were bright, minimal equipped rooms which are multifunctional with experimental designs, photographs, and unconventional things. That's what became visible in their poster motifs, for which the photographs they created serve as metaphors for creativity.

FINAL SOLUTION
By elaborating a style guide together with a lookbook the team was not only able to create a well-conceived corporate identity, but also achieved the exact aesthetics and design they had in mind for RAUM. In several photo shoots they created fitting photographs that were used for posters and the website.

[R]

Zusammenarbeiten und zusammen arbeiten.

RAUM
Sanderheinrichsleitenweg 20
97074 Würzburg
www.raum.de

Tríada is from the new collection by fashion designer Javier Lafuente. It wants to evoke the female gender symbology by representing the figure of the upside down triangle. Geometric shapes, based on the triangle, are what shape the female figure in all his garments.

Design agency **Fetén Studio**
Design **Sara Bautista, Alex De La Fuente**
Client **Javier Lafuente**

Tríada

TASK
The client wanted an identity that could bring the same feeling of his clothes to printed media and website, and also recognizable.

INSPIRATIONS & CONCEPTS
The color palette of the collection and the geometric shapes gave the team the key for the brand. All the subtle lines and perfect symmetry were both paths to follow and something remarkable. Automatically the team was influenced by Bauhaus and constructivism.

FINAL SOLUTION
Finally the team ended up with a sans serif light logotype that plays with the symmetry. Out of the logotype they made a monogram that plays with the "A" to bring a downside triangle to the game. Colors speak for the brand with personality and accuracy. The font choice is Hurme Geometric sans combined with designer petition, Courier new.

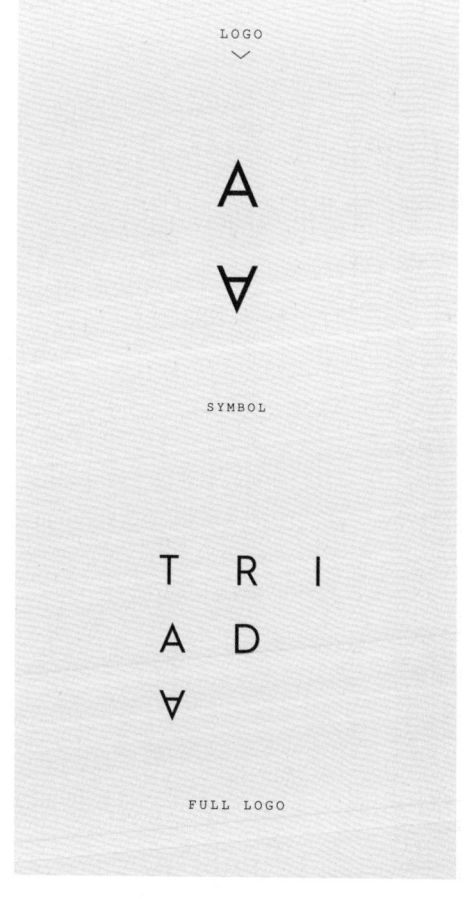

Established in 2012, Everest Isles is a brand dedicated to creating bold swimwear and nautical inspired sportswear of superior quality. With finest luxury, technical performance textiles, and industrial components, the products are designed for modern men and built for an active modern lifestyle.

Design agency **Studio Newwork**
Design **Ryotatsu Tanaka, Ryo Kumazaki, Hitomi Ishigaki**
Client **Everest Isles**

Everest Isles

TASK
Studio Newwork was assigned to create the brand identity system including logotype, symbol, stationery, woven label, hang tag, lookbook, and website.

INSPIRATIONS & CONCEPTS
Although the team found inspiration in classic nautical terms attached to sailing, their approach to Everest Isles's branding was focused on clean urban design with modern color palette to reflect innovative fits and refined construction of their products.

FINAL SOLUTION
The logotype was designed in a bold sans-serif typeface with diagonal ends of strokes in letter E, L, and T. The symbol was designed based on vintage semaphore illustration. In semaphore flag signals, it says EI, the initials of Everest Isles. Uneven ink stamp and embossing stamp add a humanistic sensibility to the clean presentation and give a subtle but distinctive character to the brand. The lookbook was bound by yacht cordage used in grand prix yacht racing as well as their swim trunks.

EVEREST
ISLES

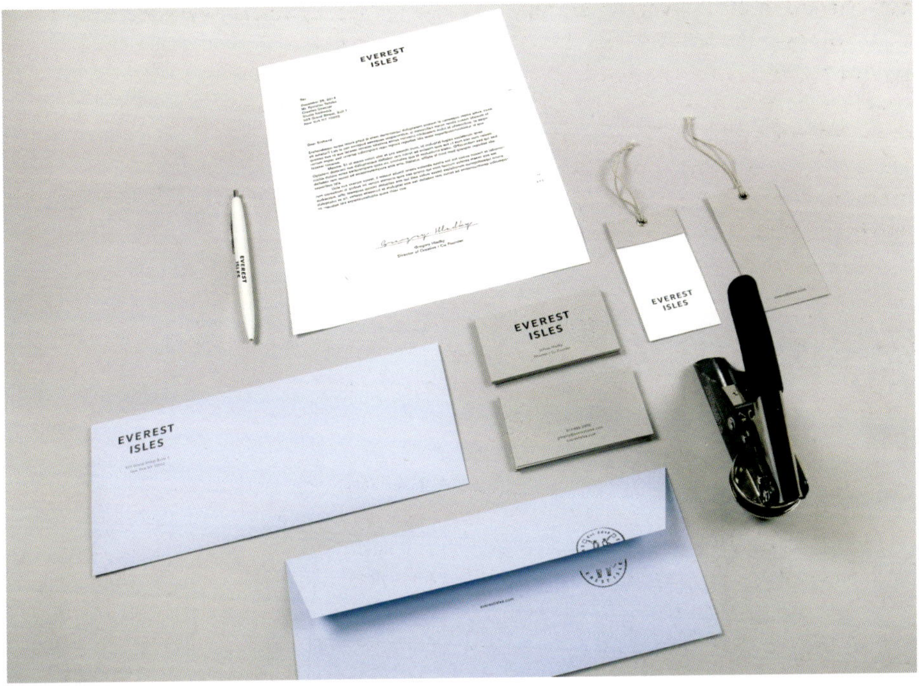
EVEREST
ISLES
EVEREST
ISLES
EVEREST
ISLES
EVEREST
ISLES
EVEREST
ISLES

EVEREST
ISLES
EVEREST
ISLES

A newly launched brand positioned as an interactive agency focused on flexible, friendly, and functional solutions in a global market.

Design agency **La Nacional Estudio Mexicano**
Design **Berenice Luna, Tomás Salazar**
Art design **Israel Viveros, Tomás Salazar**
Client **DNA Agency**

DNA Agency

TASK
The goal was to achieve a clean and friendly brand image in order to make the brand easily recognized in the international market.

INSPIRATIONS & CONCEPTS
The concept was created from the connection between the connectivity of the digital media and the human DNA, resulting in a synergy between human sense and the digital values. That meant the humanization of the digital media.

FINAL SOLUTION
The final solution was a simple dots pattern, with a vibrant blue palette and a clear and readable type, generating a clean composition. Personality was given by the dot on the last Y letter.

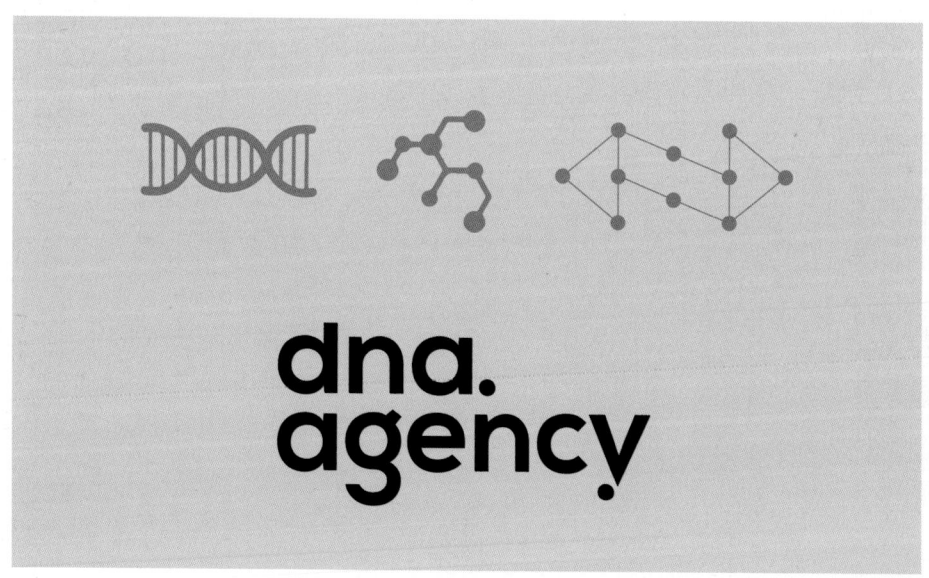

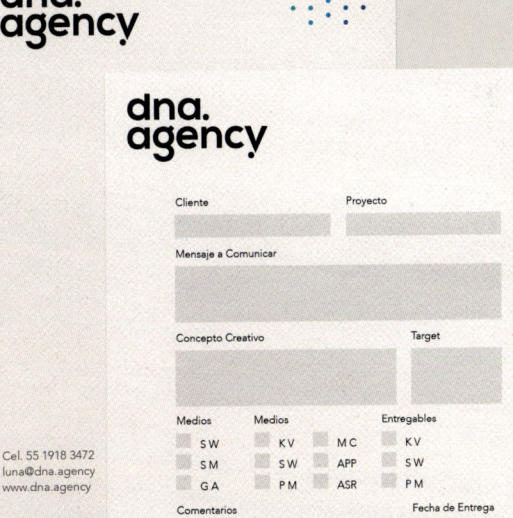

The Canadian Ski Museum is a lost cabin located in Ottawa, Ontario, Canada.

Design **Eliane Cadieux**
Client **The Canadian Ski Museum** (School Project)

Canadian Ski Museum

TASK

The brief was to choose a subject and create a branding around it. The designer is passionate about skiing and when she saw the website of the Canadian Ski Museum she was shocked. She decided to rebrand it with a new style to speak to the ski community (young and old people).

INSPIRATIONS & CONCEPTS

The inspiration and the concept came from the Canadian mountains and landscapes. The only colors in a winter landscape of Canada are white and black. Everything is simple when you ski. The designer wanted to infuse the feeling into the brand.

FINAL SOLUTION

The brand is simple, clear, and represents the Canadian history of skiing. The logo is actually a part of the leaf of the Canadian flag. The designer played with the icon and a bold and serious typography. She applied the logo on 3 brochures for exhibitions, stationary, website, and a tuque.

MUSÉE DU SKI
CANADIEN

CANADIAN
SKI MUSEUM

79

A family run company founded by Wilhelm Køltzow in 1916. Køltzow has been supplying top quality seafood, meat, and game to professional kitchens for almost 100 years.

Design **Gøril Torske, Geir Lysbakken, Sigrid Pfanzelter, Kine Ugelstad**
Photography **Veslemøy Vråskar(Palookaville), Mathias Fossum**
Client **BAMA Storkjøkken(Køltzow)**

Køltzow Identity

TASK
When Køltzow recently joined BAMA Kitchen Services, their visual expression was felt outdated, and strongly in need of an upgrade to match BAMA's newly developed one – whilst retaining their own unique personality.

INSPIRATIONS & CONCEPTS
Quality is a key word for Køltzow produce, so the approach was to focus on the "origin" of the products: the revered fjords and mountains of Norway known for its natural fertility and freshness. This was encapsulated in a monogram and imagery that carefully complimented the BAMA identity.

FINAL SOLUTION
The new symbol reflects the origins of the products; the K of Køltzow is tilted so that, when put together with the W (from the original brand name W. Køltzow), they form a mountain range – set above the horizontal line of the sea.

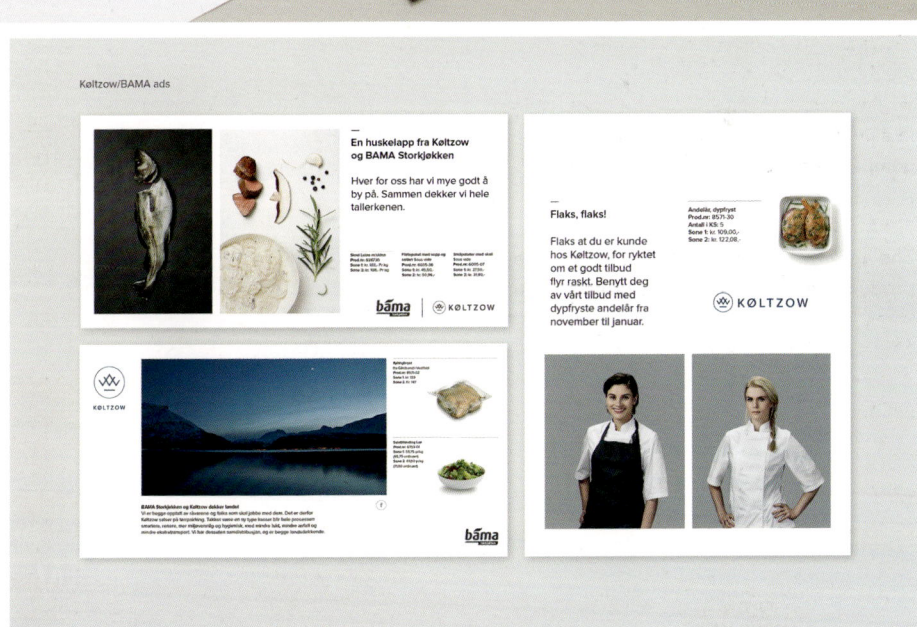

84

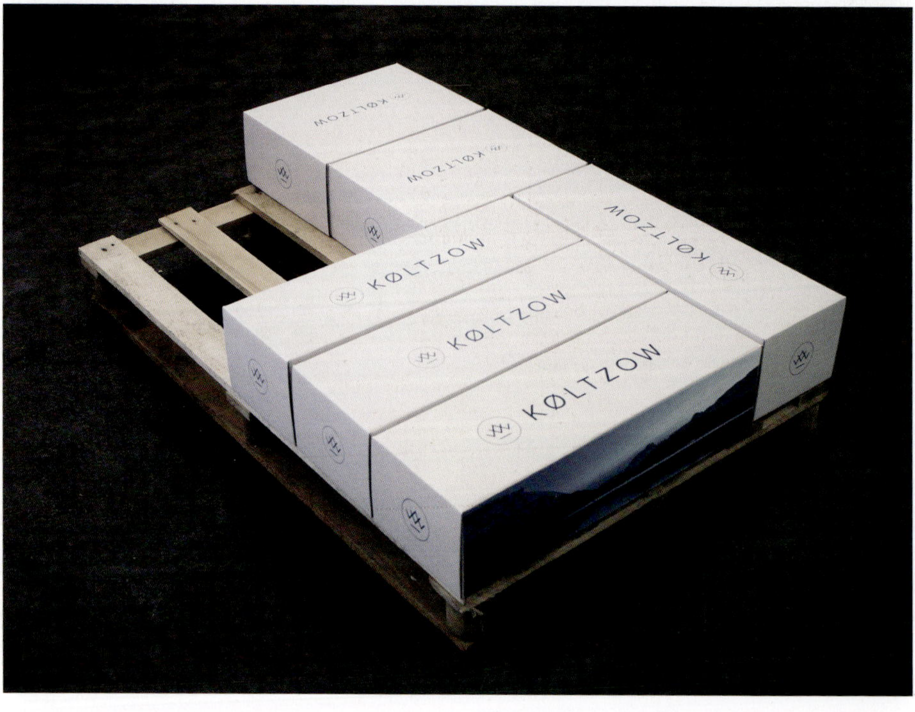

Soil Nature Equip is a small outdoor store in Coquiltam, British Columbia, Canada. The store features premium quality outdoor and lifestyle products like Arc'teryx, Patagonia, Snow Peak, Vibram, Ibex, La Sportiva, Scarpa, Big Agnes, Nobis, etc. Bobo and Tin started Soil in December 2011 and it's all about reuniting people with nature.

Design **Eliane Cadieux**
Client **Soil Nature Equip**

Soil Nature Equip

TASK
The designer was assigned to create their corporate identity, as well as apply it on many other tools. She thus created a strong and complete vi system including logotype, fonts, color palette, and website.

INSPIRATIONS & CONCEPTS
The inspiration came from the nature of the North America. Canadian people live in a landscape of trees, lakes, and mountains.

The concept was to create this world in a brand with icon and photography.

FINAL SOLUTION
The designer developed many variations of the logotype in different colors. Different colors represent different seasons of her beautiful country. She chose bold font and scripted it to make the brand more human. And finally, the brand lives on the website.

86

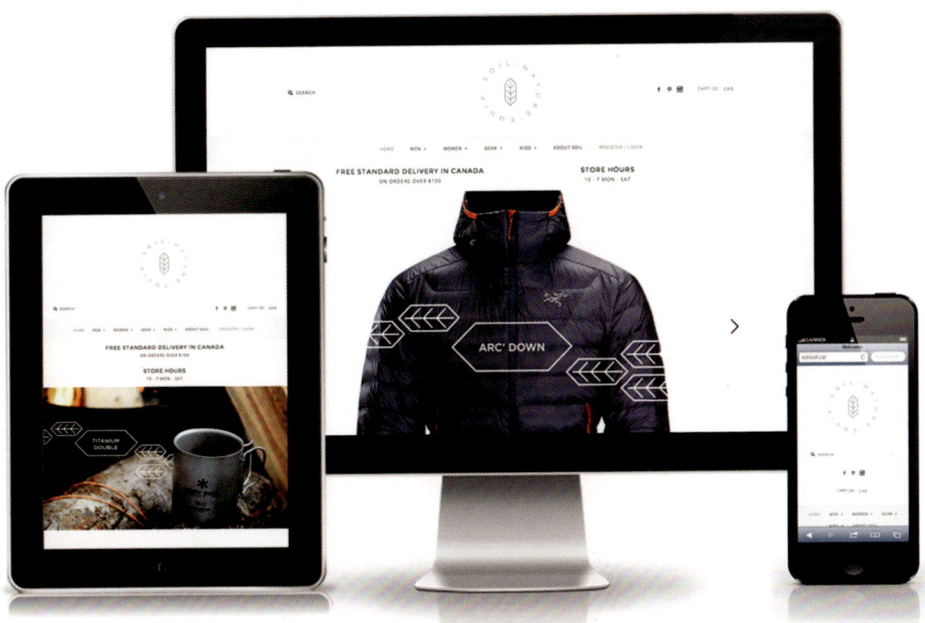

Tokyo Art Room (TAR) consists of a group of people who are passionate about increasing the number of Japanese makers (artists, designers, musicians, craftsmen, etc.) who can earn foreign currency. The members of TAR are spending all free time for this mission as they believe Japanese market will decline in the near future due to increasing global competitions with third world countries and decreasing population of the working age group in Japan.

Design agency **Enhanced Inc.**
Design **Hiromi Maeo**
Client **Zens**

Tokyo Art Room Identity

TASK
The task was the realization of the logo that changes dynamically, which embodies their services, and corresponds to each rooms using grid.

INSPIRATIONS & CONCEPTS
The inspirations and concepts included the visualization of the connection, the additive color mixing method, and the molecular structure.

FINAL SOLUTION
Structure: The square of the logo represents the individual and the room. If the logo is the molecule conjugate, the square is one of the molecules. These will link through the room. This is the beginning of connection via room (the individual and the individual, Japan and the world). The connection becomes bigger like the larger molecular structure, similar to the change into a valuable diamond by the connection of the carbon molecular.

Color: Except for black, the setting of the logo color was free. The color as the result of connection was born by color mixing. The structure and color represent the intermixing of identity via room.

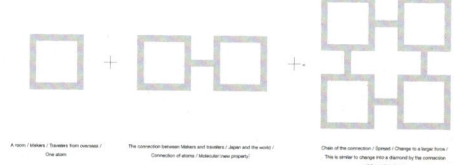

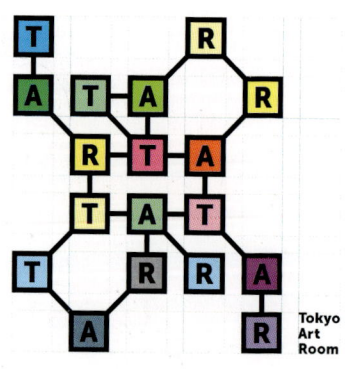

88

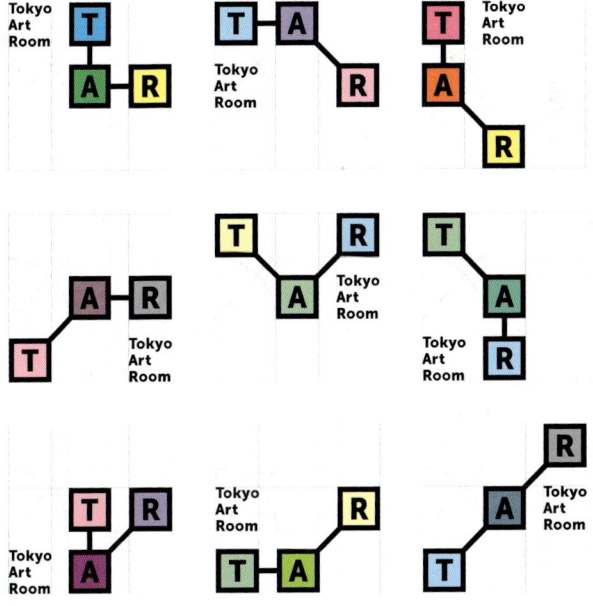

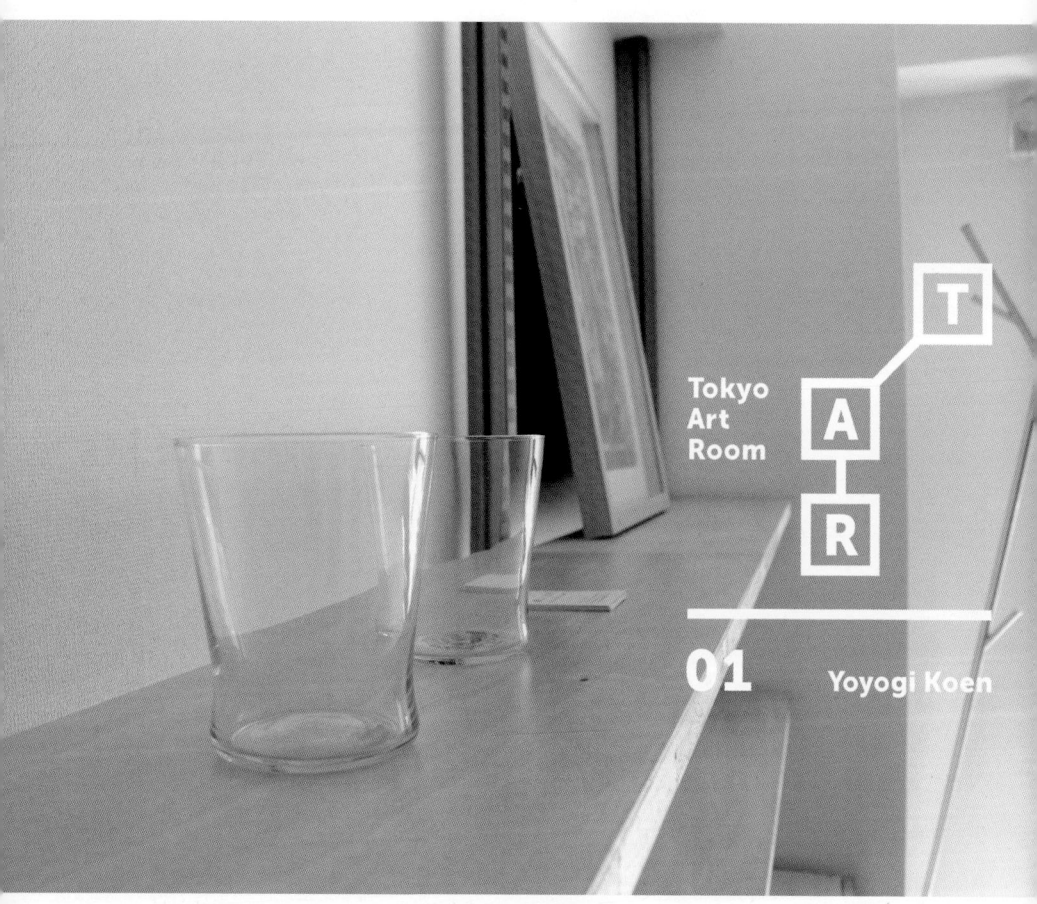

Daikin Industries Ltd. is a Japanese multinational and the world's leading company in indoor climate systems for domestic, commercial, and industrial uses. Daikin's products are focused on saving energy and reducing CO_2 emissions, such as its energy-efficient heat pump systems. Established in 1924, Daikin celebrated 90 years of success and took special consideration for innovation, sustainability, and environmental responsibility in 2014.

Design agency **Fabrica**
Graphic identity **Tomomi Maezawa**
Creative direction **Sam Baron**
Photography **Marco Zanin, Marco Furio Magliani**
Client **Daikin**

FUHA

TASK
FUHA is a multisensory artistic layout with a multitude of creative stories that give shape to air, designed by Fabrica for Daikin and presented at the 2015 Milan Furniture Fair.

INSPIRATIONS & CONCEPTS
"FU" and "HA" are two traditional Japanese onomatopoeic expressions reminiscent of the sound of human breath. "FU" recalls the sound of blowing on something to cool it, while "HA" imitates the sound of exhaling to warm something. Using this concept as their starting point, Fabrica's researchers created a setting in which the air is the designer. Through ten different installations in which air manifested its existence in the form of sound, weight, or substance, visitors came into contact with the invisible, thus turning the intangible into a physical interaction.

FINAL SOLUTION
The color palette was in a natural and earthy shade (from beige to gray) to emphasise the exhibition's focus on the materials that they had carefully chosen for each installation. There was a slight difference in the subtle movements of each set of the letters, FU and HA, because they are two different breaths. In any media, each element was composed as if there was a wind in the graphic.

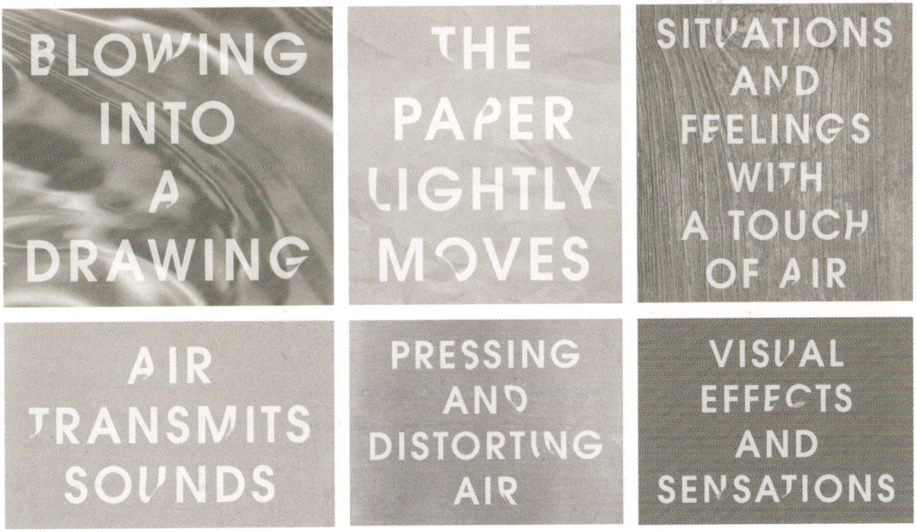

BLOWING INTO A DRAWING	THE PAPER LIGHTLY MOVES	SITUATIONS AND FEELINGS WITH A TOUCH OF AIR
AIR TRANSMITS SOUNDS	PRESSING AND DISTORTING AIR	VISUAL EFFECTS AND SENSATIONS

93

Nomo® Creative is a Taipei-based design studio founded by three designers in 2015. They were working as freelancers for many years in the creative industry, before they have decided to start their own studio together, and named it as "Nomo."

Design agency **Nomo® Creative**
Design **Yu Chien Lin, Chi Tai Lin, Chen Huang Chian**
Client **Nomo® Creative**

Nomo® Creative

TASK
The core belief of Nomo® Creative is to provide its clients practical brand design solutions. The team suggests that the core concept of design should be simple, sustainable, practical, and functional. Through design, they simplified ideas without losing the brand essence. From designing, production, to business management, they embodied the belief of Nomo® Creative, aiming to achieve their vision: to provide their clients sustainable brand value.

INSPIRATIONS & CONCEPTS
Minimalist design and the fusion between western and oriental art are their design core. Therefore they named the design studio "不毛 (bu-mao)" in Chinese and "nomo" for English, which means desolation, often used to describe barren land. Just like how they wish to explore new brand directions through uncertainties, and pursue the beauty within imperfection.

FINAL SOLUTION
To portray the mix of symbolism and calligraphy, the team reversed the Chinese character "不 (bu)" in "不毛 (bu-mao)," and created a cactus-like symbol, indirectly conveying their brand philosophy.

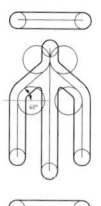 

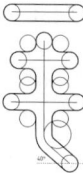 

96

Studio Maarten Deckers is the habitat of Belgium based designer and art director Maarten Deckers who creates identities, logos, books, magazines, and all kinds of digital and printed matter for clients and himself.

Design **Maarten Deckers**
Client **Studio Maarten Deckers**

Studio Maarten Deckers

TASK
Designing a corporate identity for one's own studio is not easy, especially when he/she is a designer with a tendency to constantly adjust and refine. Therefore the designer decided to create a simple and flexible design that can be easily adjusted in the future and can grow over time.

INSPIRATIONS & CONCEPTS
The elements that make up the logo are not farfetched. They are simply a combination of the first letters of the designer's first and last name combined with a cloud of imagination and placed inside a circle. The designer chose a circle as a circle is a perfect shape to him, that he can't improve or tinker with.

FINAL SOLUTION
Due to its simplicity, the logo works both as a positive and a negative shape and the designer easily switches between both versions. To make the design even more flexible, there's no fixed color palette. Only black and one spot color that changes every now and then according to the designer's taste was chosen. The designer doesn't use a fixed set of fonts either, but rather a flexible selection of fonts that blend well with the logo. The rest of his brand elements are a hodgepodge of things the designer liked as a kid: kraft paper, wood structures, stamps, and simple packaging.

| M | + | ☁ | + | D | = | 🖐 |
| MAARTEN | | IMAGINATION | | DESIGN | | |

101

Bienhecho is the market for the good local economies. Its mission is to foster responsible consumption by supporting brands and producers from the local economy, those who make good products and pursue of the common good through their commitment to the community and the environment.

Design **Olivier Rensonnet**
Client **theiouproject.com**

Bienhecho

TASK
The designer was assigned to make a logo for Bienhecho that reflects the spirit of the brand.

INSPIRATIONS & CONCEPTS
Keywords for graphic way include simple, visible, elegent, transversal, conceptual, symbolic but not mystic, fresh, fundamental, and unique.

FINAL SOLUTION
The logo of Bienhecho was made to be in great balance with all the partner brands. Soveriety is the perfect way to be visible.

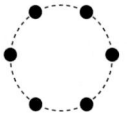
community

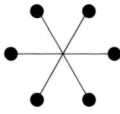
centralisation

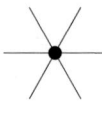
product story

font mass

symbol to integrate

BIEN
HECHO

Iis igitur est difficilius satis facere, qui se Latina scripta dicunt contemnere.

Cur in gravissimis rebus non delectet eos sermo patrius, cum idem fabellas.

BIEN
HECHO

Iis igitur est difficilius satis facere, qui se Latina scripta dicunt contemnere.

Cur in gravissimis rebus non delectet eos sermo patrius, cum idem fabellas Latinas ad verbum et Graecis expressas non inviti legant. quis enim tam inimicus paene nomini Romano est, qui Ennii Medeam aut Antiopam Pacuvii spernat aut reiciat, quod se isdem Euripidis fabulis delectari dicat, Latinas litteras oderit?

Cur in gravissimis rebus non delectet eos sermo patrius, cum idem fabellas.

Cur in gravissimis rebus non delectet eos sermo patrius, cum idem fabellas.

103

The Nordic is a fictional food truck brand offering Nordic food focused on smørrebrøds (open sandwiches), which are cheap and popular in Nordic countries and can be quickly prepared.

Design **Alexandre Pietra**
Client **The Nordic**

The Nordic Food Truck

TASK
The work was created for the designer's final exam on the theme of global street food branding, with requirements that the design should reflect not only the unique street food culture in a specific area, but also a modern design touch. Research and analysis on street food cultures were undertaken at the beginning of the design process and a Nordic food truck brand came to the designer's mind. Scandinavian design has an excellent reputation for its unfussy style and is often taken as a source of inspiration in various sectors. So it became important to create a sober and minimal design to give an authentic Scandinavian feeling.

INSPIRATIONS & CONCEPTS
The designer wanted to find elements that would speak for a Nordic style by their own. N, the first letter of Nordic; a Nordic typical house with a very identifiable roof; the North cardinal point came to his mind. The identity should be eye-catching and leave strong impression to the customers so some simplification work should be done.

FINAL SOLUTION
The designer mixed the three elements to make up the logo with both the roof of the Nordic typical house and the North cardinal point simplified into a triangle on the top of the "N." A perfectly representative monogram was thus created.

The chosen typeface is a geometric sans-serif highly spaced between letters which strengthens the qualitative side of the brand. Sans-serif typography best represents the modernity of the universe. The light weight creates a contrast between the typography and the monogram that we found in all the applications.

As for the color, black was chosen for the logo as it transmits a sense of elegance and restraint. White that represents the environment and the color of wood that gives the design more warmth were chosen as the background color. Kraft paper was used as it visually transcribes at best the spirit of wood.

Wroclove Design Festival had its second edition in May 2014. It was held at Wroclaw's Main Railway Station, which was recently restored. More than 20,000 people visited this edition, while over 150 lectures and workshops were held. The goal of the festival was to promote modern design and young designers, as well as to educate the public on the importance of good designs.

Design **Natalia Żerko**
Client **Dobrzedobrze.net**

Wroclove Design Festival 2014

TASK
The task was to design a visual identity concept for the festival as a whole and for the specific festival zones (Kids Design, Fresh Design, Urban Garden, etc.). The title of this edition was "Design: Otwarty" ("Design: Open" in English). Along with the main concept, the designer designed some of the promotional materials like posters, billboards, t-shirts, and bags.

INSPIRATIONS & CONCEPTS
The main inspiration behind the project came from two words: "open" and "space." As a design festival is an open space for education, presentation of ideas, and experience of different solutions and viewpoints, the branding needed to reflect that.

FINAL SOLUTION
The designer used the shape of an open and resizable rectangle to illustrate the concept. Using this shape and spilled typography she was able to show the theme "Design: Open." The rectangle created a space which was easily scaled to all of the branded carriers. Using two strong colors (red and blue) gave the brand enough visibility to function well in a busy city environment.

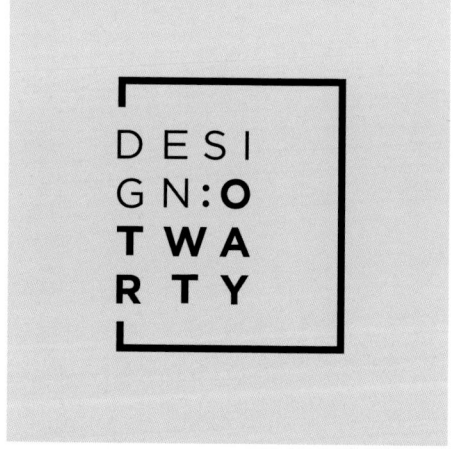

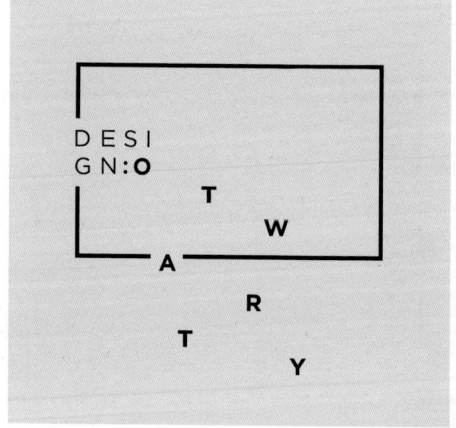

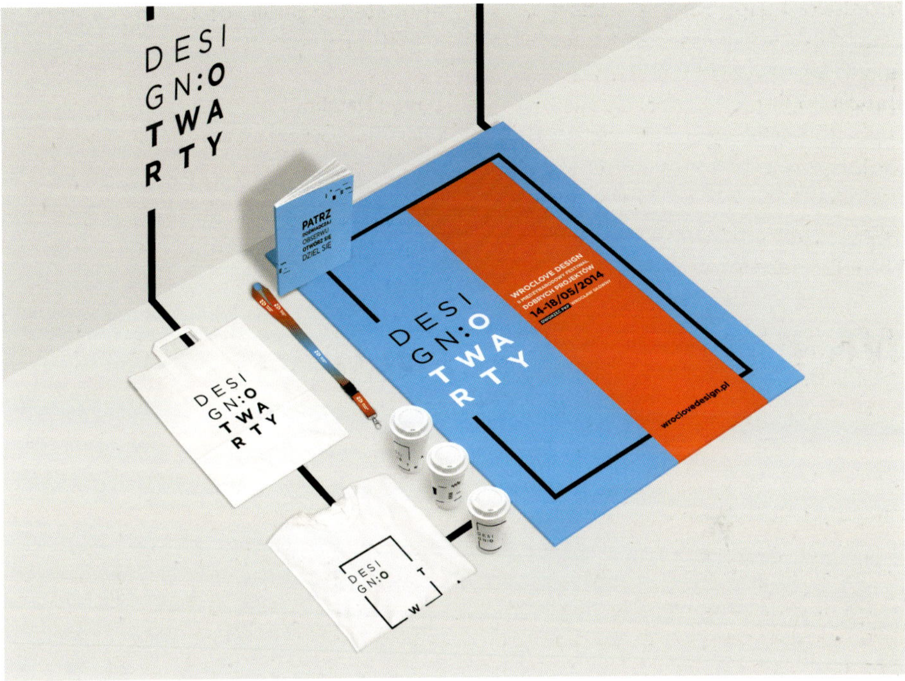

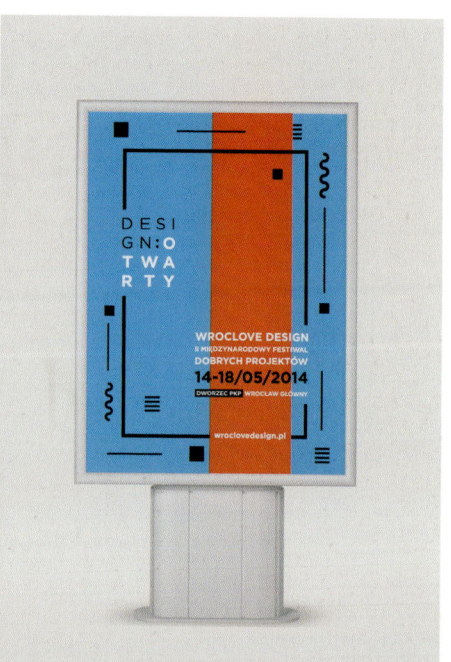

Common, Rare is an independent artful book store that offers a thoughtfully selected assortment of readings, specialized in combining new and old books.

Design **Jurate Gacionyte**
Client **Common, Rare (School project)**

Common, Rare

TASK
It is a contemporary brand that aims to gather the most exciting new publications as well as shine a light on some rescued, forgotten, or overlooked treasures from the past. With a strong emphasis on quality both in content and aesthetics, it really becomes a showcase. The design should reflect such a quality of the book store.

INSPIRATIONS & CONCEPTS
Inspiration for the identity came through looking at various aspects and elements of books: contemporary, experimental, or traditional publications; the materials and the aesthetics of books; the experience of reading, etc.

FINAL SOLUTION
"Common" and "rare" are book terms. They are a part of book language, and became part of the brand's visual language. The color scheme came from the reading experience. Black text on off-white pages (particularly aged yellow paper in old books). A supplementary accent color which emerged from the tradition of edge-coloring of book pages (this very approach was reflected on the business cards) was added – red was chosen as one of the more common and classic. The primary typeface is a contemporary sans serif – GT Haptik, paired with a secondary Arno, a modern typeface inspired by Italian Renaissance. The whole identity is structured combining opposing ideas: modern and traditional, playful and elegant, forward-looking and nostalgic.

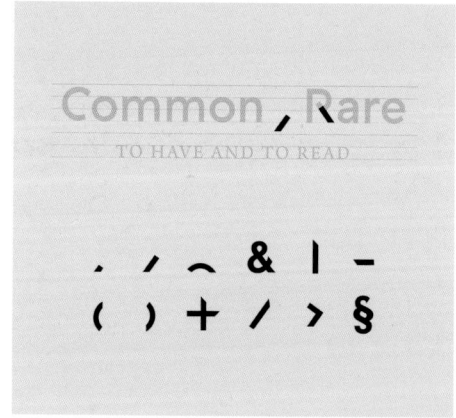

Apofenia is a brand for the team's very own studio, meant to be used for self promotion, and most importantly, to express the way they think, the approach they use to handle the projects they choose to engage with, and the way they like things to be done.

Design **Apofenia**
Client **Apofenia**

Apofenia Studio

TASK
To the team, the brand was to be built upon something meaningful, and something people could relate to. They wanted it to be a clear definition of why they do things. To them, it must not be a straight forward thing, but should rather be out there for people to dig it.

INSPIRATIONS & CONCEPTS
Every person has a built-in ability for pattern recognition, and it is so sharp that one can even recognize patterns out of random data. Take a constellation for instance, the stars are randomly set in the sky but yet people connect the dots, it doesn't have a meaning but it makes sense to us. This is a phenomenon called Apophenia. Here in the studio the team used it to make connections where there were none, to organize chaos, and to make the world intelligible. To them, it is useful to create ideas in their clients' mind, and to set the dots for them to connect.

FINAL SOLUTION
The logotype was set on the team's own custom font called Epifanía, a bold semi-serif typeface with a strong feeling of roman characters and a signature capital letter A. The letter A also became an icon accompanied by the full name around it resembling a circle, set in François Rappo's Theinhardt typography.

"We believe coffee and art can tell stories." Nidificate is a fictional brand created by four students for their diploma in graphic design in their final year project exhibition. It is a branding project for a conceptual café.

Design **Lee Wai Lun, Lim Fei Zun, Leong Kah Fai**
Illustration **Foo Chen En**
Client **Nidificate (Self-initiated)**

Nidificate

TASK
The task was to create a fictional brand including designs of corporate identity, collateral materials, TV commercials, the website, and exhibition booth.

INSPIRATIONS & CONCEPTS
Nidificate is a café, art gallery, and concept store all in one. It's a place that allows people to savor coffee and art. The objective is to provide a warm, serene environment, and to offer an inspirational atmosphere. The literal meaning of Nidificate is "to build a nest." The team envisioned a timeless and artistic space where people are able to act freely and comfortably, and wished Nidificate would be peacefully heard through the language of simplicity. Therefore, they emphasized on the values of natural and minimalism.

FINAL SOLUTION
Using the combination of neutral colors and wood texture to bring out the hand-crafted aesthetic of the brand and create a visual consistency in all collateral materials. The hand drawn illustrations evoke the feeling of natural and exquisite, adding an artistic touch to the overall design.

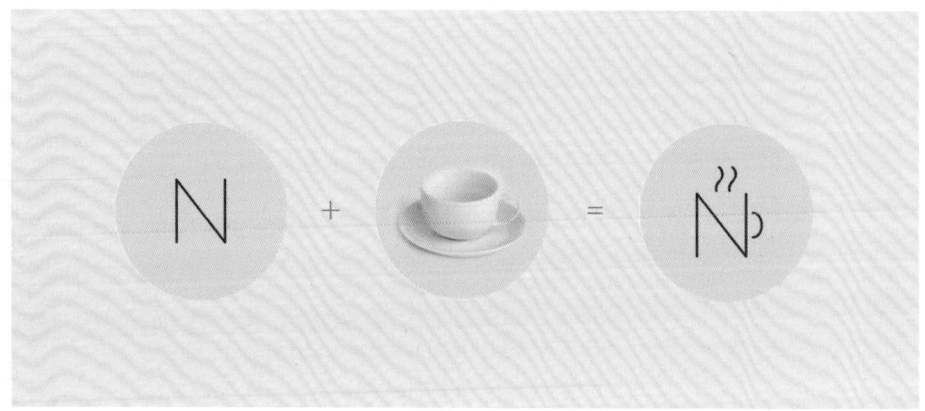

Roost, a hair salon in Tsuzuki-ku, Yokohama-city, is located in a quiet residential area with a park that is filled with nature and away from the downtown near the Center Minami station.

Design **Masaomi Fujita**
Client **Hair salon "Roost"**

Hair Salon "Roost"

TASK
At the request of the hair salon, the team needed to provide a sign, shop card, business card, stamp card, and a leaflet for them. But firstly, they needed to design a symbolic mark which represented the concept of the hair salon.

INSPIRATIONS & CONCEPTS
The logo for Roost features "O" that resembles the bird nest. The logo represents the team's hope that the hair salon will be a place where customers can feel relaxed and at home, a place that customers want to go back to, and a place loved by many people in the area. The birds that are looking around, peeking out from the nests, express the anxiety and excitement people often have when they leave a hair salon with a new hairstyle. The logo embodies the salon's message that, with new hairstyle, Roost's customers will be filled with new hopes and fly away to the future.

FINAL SOLUTION
By giving a storyline to the birds in the Os, the team succeeded to widen the meaning of the logo and make it applicable for various uses. A sleeping bird was created for the use on the concept board in the salon. For the leaflet, the team used photos that were taken in Northern Europe, as they thought that the clear and translucent quality of those photos could emphasize the clean image of the salon. They also gave the salon's original cards and tools a wood texture in order to keep the overall design "natural."

Broodje van Eigen Deeg is a French bakery located in the Netherlands. With a unique concept in making their own bread dough, they are specialized in French bread, pastry, and confectionery. They prepare dough with respect for the ancient craft and select pure ingredients without additives. Their always freshly baked bread is inspired by the French tradition.

Design **Jeroen van Eerden**
Client **Broodje van Eigen Deeg**

Broodje van Eigen Deeg

TASK
The task was to create a full corporate branding for Broodje van Eigen Deeg including a full communication and marketing strategy with all needed visuals and other designs for their business. The designer has been working on the following elements for their branding completion:
compile and finalize the key corporate messages and the overall communication and marketing strategies, identify and create graphic elements that would carry through all corporate communications: web, print, documents, PDF, etc., and create a logo usage guideline manual.

INSPIRATIONS & CONCEPTS
The designer took inspiration from the old hand-crafted bread makers. In the concepts he also included the French element and used the capital B in different approaches. Elements like wheat, bread, craftwork, and France are all used as concepts during this project.

FINAL SOLUTION
The final logo mark was also the designer's first logo concept: a capital B with a loaf in the middle of it. The designer used the negative space of the shape to create this smart and beautiful mark. After the mark was set, he added the colors based on the color of baked bread, next with a clean but suiting typography in all black. Also the message of a bakery with hand-crafted bread was clear and obvious for the audience to understand. The client was happy with the overall visual feeling it was giving.

Boulangerie 41 is a half-French half-Mexican patisserie and bakery based in Mexico City, dedicated to produce high-quality and healthy meals for customers. Their vision is to bring Mexico a refined, yet modern, coffee place with an open pastry kitchen. The menu is composed of modern French-style pastries along with sweet flavors and local influences.

Design **Nephews**
Client **Boulangerie 41**

Boulangerie 41

TASK
The task was to create a new concept, name, and unique color palette for the patisserie, to create a design solution that will deliver high visual impact for the target, and to provide not only a logo but a complete branding system for interior design, packaging, digital media, and advertising.

INSPIRATIONS & CONCEPTS
The design was inspired by traditional French bakeries, baby blue color (for a fresh start), French handmade tile, mix of baroque and rococo elements with simple modern elements, and Reina typeface.

FINAL SOLUTION
The team named the bakery as the simple form in French "Boulangerie" and took the number from the first location address number #41. In order to have a short name for it, B41 came up.

At the beginning, the team chose Bodoni, a serif typeface that is very elegant and represents all the French details they were looking for. When they extracted the letter "B" they found that the icon alone needed more character. So they chose Reina Typeface, a more ornamented, sweet, and bold typeface with decorative accolades that helped manage the composition.

The team used black for the color of the logo as they always use black as the first color to start. Other colors used include baby blue that represents trust and reliability, and none of the coffee shops around had ever used, and light brown that triggers the impression of bread, recycle paper, and the selected furniture for the place.

The illustration of French-based tile came together to do the synergy. All branding and collateral were created using simple materials such as kraft paper, ceramic plates, stamps, as well as hand-painted wall graphics and store signages.

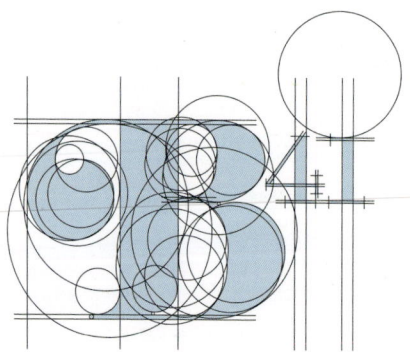

125

Barba Bird is a hair salon based in Poland, providing excellent hairdressing services.

Design **Dawid Cmok**
Client **Barba Bird**

Barba Bird Identity

TASK
Create a logo for Barba Bird that would be easily recognized and distinguished among other brands in the world.

INSPIRATIONS & CONCEPTS
Scissors that are essentials in a hair salon, bird that comes from the name of the brand name.

FINAL SOLUTION
The designer combined the scissors and the wings of a bird to create a logo with a rebellious touch and modern look. Within his work the designer also created logotype variants, letterheads, envelopes, visiting cards, folders, patterns, identity book, hairdressing accessories, etc.

 +  +

The Code Showroom was established in 1996 by a group of Hungarian professionals with experience in furniture manufacturing. The predecessor of the current 500-square-meter store in Nagymező Street was brühl&co in Andrássy út, which operated in the main street of Budapest from 2003. The Code Showroom indicates the renewed philosophy even in its name, according to which design should be consciously integrated into our daily lives.

Design **Kovács Levente**
Client **Code Showroom**

Code Showroom Redesign Concept

TASK
Rethink the conception of the existing logo and create a more talkative and interpretable version based on the philosophy of the company. Not only the logo, the whole website and its structure were reconsidered as well. Additionally, the designer created personalized business card, postcard, and envelope.

INSPIRATIONS & CONCEPTS
To the designer, the current identity of the company does not reflect well what the company represents. He read the history of company and imagined a more modern identity based on it. He paid much attention on the philosophy of the company. To him, the design should be consciously integrated into our daily lives.

FINAL SOLUTION
Based on the concept, the designer created a brand new logo with a hidden furniture and the hidden monogram of the company.

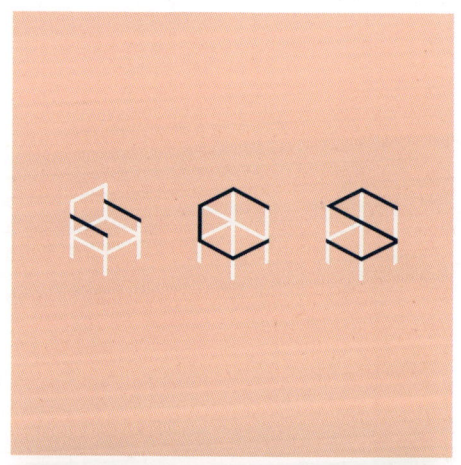

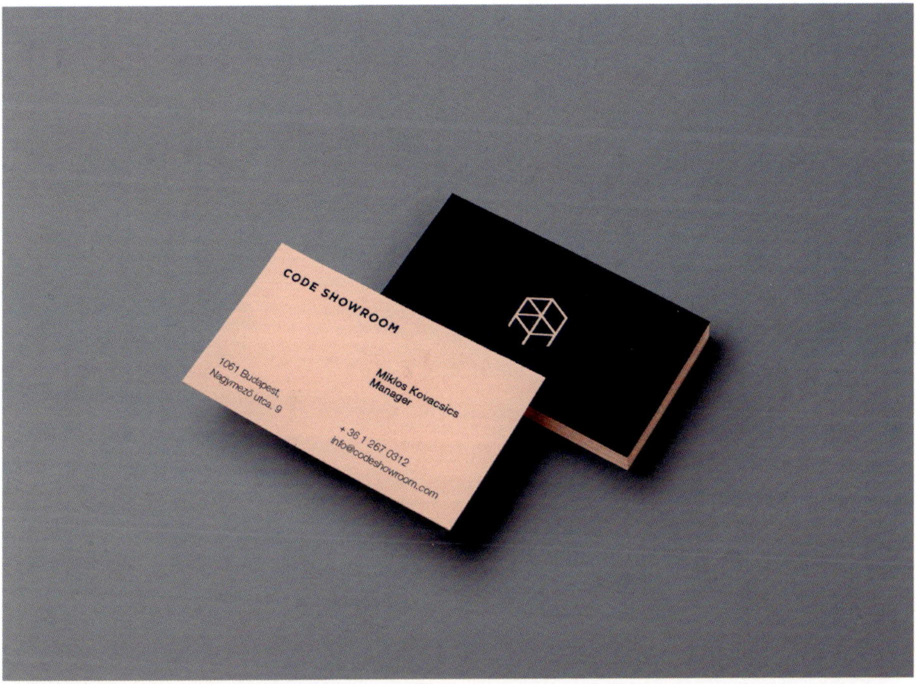
CODE SHOWROOM
Miklos Kovacsics
Manager
1061 Budapest,
Nagymező utca. 9
+ 36 1 267 0312
info@codeshowroom.com

CODE SHOWROOM
TISZTELT ÜGYFELÜNK!

Caramello is a visionary, capable of recognizing the potentials of any space and blending it with its clients' desires and dreams to change reality. The results of its work are architectural and interior design projects with a tailor-made touch and a unique texture signature.

Design **WonderID**
Client **Caramello**

Caramello

TASK
A talented architect contacted the design team to develop the concept, experience, and visual identity of her new firm from scratch. Her wish was to have an identity deeply connected with her values, inspirations, and beliefs. The challenge was to deeply understand the brand and translate it into its personality, logo, and stationery.

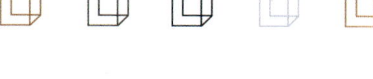

INSPIRATIONS & CONCEPTS
The client's style and the sensation of delight that invaded anyone who visited her projects were the team's main inspirations. They were flabbergasted with her incredible skill to unite natural textures and the careful manner in which she took care of each client. The team decided to translate it through an inviting and elegant language.

FINAL SOLUTION
The choice of the name was the team's first completion. Caramello was chosen because it's the architect's signature color and also an exquisite sweet. Both meanings bring the warmth and coziness that the brand wants its clients to experience. Minimalism and sophistication, added with dazzling colors and the subtraction of lines were the team's recipe to create Caramello's identity.

Mariana Bottini
mariana@caramello.arq.br
55 11 95718 2579
R. Cônego Eugênio Leite 273
Pinheiros - São Paulo
www.caramello.arq.br

Shimada Co., Ltd., an old firm established in 1921 and based in Nishiyodogawa-ku Osaka city, sells furniture materials and interior materials, as well as makes furniture. In response to the company's consultation regarding CI renewal upon the office relocation, tegusu established CI and a guideline for use of it and designed signatures and business cards.

Design **Masaomi Fujita**
Client **Shimada Co., Ltd.**

Shimada Co., Ltd.

TASK
The client demanded the team to represent the company's following three policies: provide every employee with a feeling of happiness, grow with customers and affiliate to offer innovative services, always contribute to society.

These policies led the team to the key words including confidence, conscientious, partnership, history and tradition, and experience. Based on these key words, two specific motifs were embedded into the identity of design.

INSPIRATIONS & CONCEPTS
The first is "seal and signature." Japan has traditionally used a seal to express that a document, both business and public, or a bankbook is authorized. Thus, a seal can be said as a symbol of "credit" and "trust." This inspired the team to infuse Shimada's succession of almost 100-year history and its determination to achieve the three policies with a forward-looking attitude in the motif of a seal. The second is "a structural object such as a box or a frame." Tegusu chose frames and white boxes because they are associated with an idea that decorative laminate and furniture materials offer "new value" and "colors" to a space or décor,

and that motif suggests that the company "quickens something incomplete."

FINAL SOLUTION
The symbol the team created consists of the combination of the above and arranged Chinese characters for "Shimada (島田)." The logo forms an impression of a square seal, a typical shape of corporate seals, having all characters including alphabets fit inside the square. The guideline specifies the margins to be secured when the logo is used and all samples of color patterns to be used other than its basic color, to unify the corporate image.

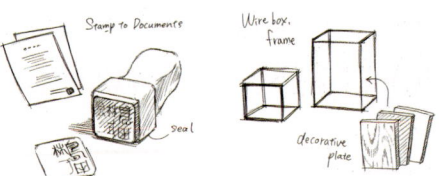

132

SHIMADA
SHIMADA
SHIMADA
SHIMADA
SHIMADA
SHIMADA
SHIMADA
SHIMADA
SHIMADA

SHIMADA
代表取締役
島田博史
SHIMADA HIROSHI
島田株式会社
SHIMADA

Established in 2000, Nolla Nolla is a Finnish high-end furniture manufacturer serving some of the most demanding residential and commercial clients with bespoke furniture and interiors. It manufactures a range of tables, chairs, and lamps, but also precision fits interiors on location, for its most demanding clients. Its furniture designs express Finnish simplicity and functionality.

Design agency **Proxy**
Design **Dan Fitzsimmons, Gernor Preslmayer**
Creative direction **Aapo Bovellan, Gernot Preslmayer**
Photography **Proxy, Pixart**
Client **Nolla Nolla**

Nolla Nolla

TASK
Led by a new partner, Nolla Nolla intends to expand across Europe. They required a new, global brand identity to position them among the high-end furniture brands. The new brand identity system needed to communicate the company's uncompromising focus on the best materials and the superior craftsmanship, both unique differentiations in a mass production market.

INSPIRATIONS & CONCEPTS
Inspired by the name Nolla Nolla – "zero zero" in Finnish, the identity was built around the concept of "origin," the geometric starting point of all precision measurements. From there, a geometric identity system was born. Organized into rational, grid-based structures, all information is secondary to the hero imagery of Nolla Nolla products.

FINAL SOLUTION
Nolla Nolla brand identity was built on the idea of "Craft and Precision." The logotype is two zeros, with two N letters hidden within. The identity system is minimal and typographic, based on Simplon by Swiss Typefaces. The brand identity was designed to be etched on products as a seal of quality, and express both online and furniture catalogues.

136

The incorporation of workers to become something bigger (in the studio's case, at first, only two people) was the main idea behind the brand. That's why the name indústria inc. was chosen – it means industry in portuguese.

Design agency **Indústria inc.**
Design **Caio Orio, Victor Pires**
Photography **Lucas Karam**
Client **Indústria inc.**

Ind Inc. Self Identity

TASK
The task was to create the studio identity translating its values, goals, and beliefs while bringing a sophisticated and contemporary feel.

INSPIRATIONS & CONCEPTS
The team was inspired by modernist, minimal graphic designers such as Alexandre Wollner and Almir Mavignier. The concept behind the identity was the factory shapes and forms.

FINAL SOLUTION
The final solution was to use basic shapes such as lines and circles, the absence of color, and shades of grey. In the end, everything needed to be simple.

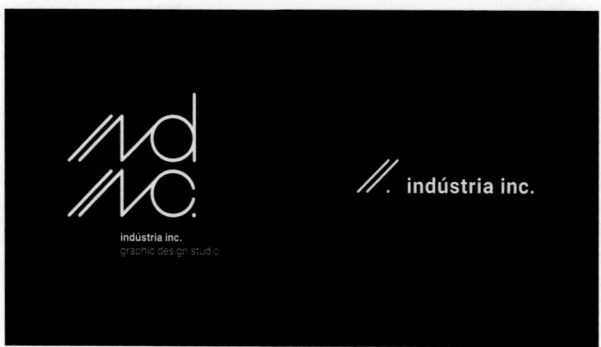

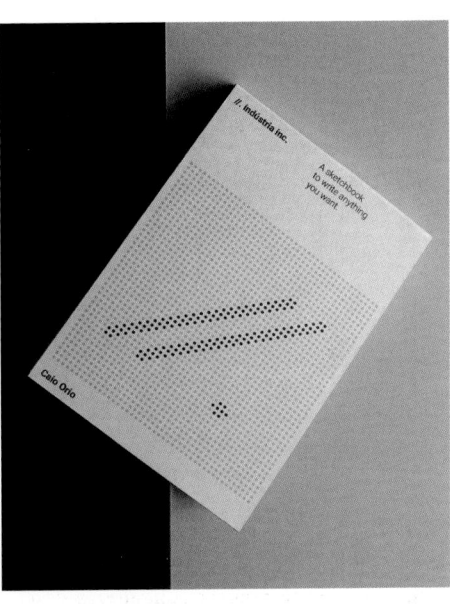
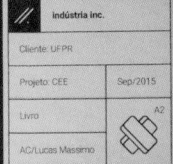

An architectural studio with innovative approach and equipped with cutting-edge technology. MOTIV specializes in producing highly detailed photorealistic or artistic visualizations, digital animations, and special effects. It is a one-stop shop and provides anything you may need from conception throughout the whole creative production process. As a multi-awarded studio, MOTIV has been working with a range of large clients from across the world.

Design agency **Negation Studio**
Design **Patryk Hardziej,**
Patrycja Podkościelny
Photography **Patrycja Podkościelny**
Client **MOTIV**

MOTIV

TASK
Client wanted to change the whole identity including the name, logo, stationery, brochures, and website. As a studio with international offices in France, Australia, and Maldives they needed to create a constant look and feeling. After all, MOTIV wanted to mark their position on international area of highly specialized architectural and CGI studio.

INSPIRATIONS & CONCEPTS
The main inspiration was the "space" and everything in common like astronauts, planets, space ships, and stars.

FINAL SOLUTION
Negation Studio designed very elegant and well executed branding, combining technical aspects of graphic design with illustration in different proportions. The basis of everything was the logo – an elegant "M" monogram designed with many lines, which optically create three dimensional sign. Every part of the new logo was mathematical analyzed and contains golden proportions. The leading color is sophisticated, metallic copper which appears almost on every single element of branding. The key visual is based on a set of unique, artistic illustrations.

+48 693 468 317
PAWEL@MOTIV-STUDIO.COM
WWW.MOTIV-STUDIO.COM
MOTIV

MOTIV

Edgeboard produces hand made chopping boards with a special feature: an edge which could be used to gather and slide chopped food off. The edge prevents the inevitable spill associated with traditional flat boards and becomes the key focus of the brand through naming and application.

Design **Maud**
Client **Edgeboard**

Edgeboard

TASK
The task included new identity, packaging, and print for Edgeboard, while the aim was to create a brand that truly reflects the product and its selling point, and hopefully creates an "aha!" moment that makes an identity stand out to the customers.

INSPIRATIONS & CONCEPTS
The brandmark will be based on the edge feature.

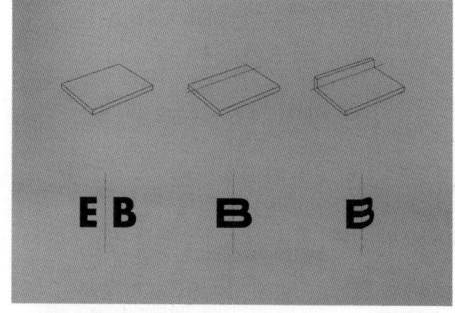

FINAL SOLUTION
The final logo is combined by the initials of "Edge" and "Board," and can be fully revealed when placed around a corner. The natural anti-bacterial, sustainable wood sourced from the Byron Shire was also used throughout packaging and stationery further adding to the tactile impact of the product.

AHK is the worldwide network of German Chambers of Commerce, with 44,000 member companies all over the world.

Design agency **H3L Studio**
Design **Luciano Geoffroy, Horacio Lardiés**
Client **AHK Argentina**

100 Años AHK Argentina

TASK
Branding project for AHK Argentina's 100th Anniversary and corporate image refreshment based on the development of a new isotype. The new brand's identity would be used in different items.

INSPIRATIONS & CONCEPTS
The identity system represents the integration of the concepts of innovation, professional training, and sustainability as the central aspects of this anniversary. The strategy was based on the idea that human bonding changes the sense of time as a straight line for an infinite future.

FINAL SOLUTION
The final logo reflects the concepts of time and bonds, implying a modern idea of time strictly associated with progress. The idea behind the development's discourse is a straight line that moves forward without any limits, technology or speed.

Pop Shop is a fictional store that creates gourmet pops in a variety of flavors ranging from fruity to even alcoholic. Every pop is "made with love" through an emphasis on fresh ingredients and a made-from-scratch philosophy.

Design **Weston Doty**
Client **Pop Shop (School project)**

Pop Shop

TASK
Pop Shop is aimed towards an adult audience, which calls for a friendly yet more mature design solution. As a school assignment, the task was to design a visual identity for Pop Shop including logo, business cards, stationery, menu, employee uniform, promotional materials, as well as product photography.

INSPIRATIONS & CONCEPTS
The aesthetics of craft and playfulness were reflected in the system through typography, colors, and physical materials. Natural and hand-made products were branded in an urban and upscale way.

FINAL SOLUTION
A custom logotype was created for Pop Shop. The rounded stencil letterforms refer to process and craftiness. The vertical strokes in the letters were made to imitate popsicle sticks. Pop Shop's symbol represents a heart, created by two overlapping popsicles. This mark was inspired by Pop Shop's slogan "made with love," and its values of sharing and togetherness. The mark is strong enough to stand on its own and to be applied to multiple materials.

Pop Shop's brand color palette was directly inspired by the ingredients it uses. Strawberry red and blueberry blue, two distinct colors strike a balance between warm and cool. When printed on white paper, the red, white, and blue scheme is also patriotic, which conjures up feelings of summertime — the best time to eat a popsicle.

Moon Fox is a new line of women's lingerie made for contemporary woman's intimates that combines unique designs and comfortable fabrics. It stands for every girl that loves her life, her freedom and is hungry for adventures, who is controversial but never reckless. The main target of the brand is girls from 18 to 30 years old from a upper middle class who express what they love and stand for through their styles.

Design **Oscar Bastidas**
Client **Moon Fox - Geraldine Alarcon**

Moon Fox

TASK
The challenge was creating a brand that was elegant and Avant Garde at the same time, with simple lines to make it easy to recall for the costumers.

INSPIRATIONS & CONCEPTS
The name "Moon Fox" is definitely a strong and powerful concept by itself. The fox is a silent and lonely animal when it comes to hunt his prey, with his elegant features and smart temper it symbolizes sensuality and mystery. The moon shows a different face every night, but it lingers on. These two night elements convey and complete each other in a perfect way.

FINAL SOLUTION
Graphic synthesis of a fox through robust geometric shapes: the fox watches his prey with serene attitude, waiting for something definitive to pass. The moon is the fox's tail, coexisting harmoniously in one modern element, where elegance and simplicity play a leading role. The logo lives on two secondary colors looking to offset the power of black, which are blue and peach.

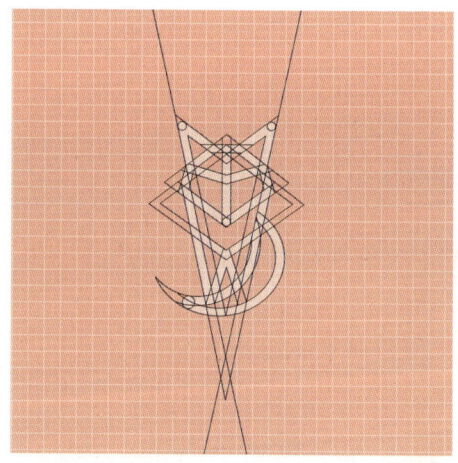

The Athens LGBTQ Community has its own voice. "Color Youth" is a colorful company of friends with a sole aim to fight sexual discrimination and inform the LGBTQ community about its rights.

Design **Maritina Laskaridou**
Client **the Athens LGBTQ community**

Color Youth – the Athens LGBTQ Community

TASK
The task was to design a logo so as to express dynamism, joy, and optimism for anything unique and different.

INSPIRATIONS & CONCEPTS
For the logo redesign the team was inspired from values such as equality, freedom, and unity.

FINAL SOLUTION
At first sight five categories of people can be seen. If looked closer, five fingers, one human hand can be found. Each entity-finger stands for a letter from LGBTQ and reflects diversity and equality. What the team aimed to show is that, like every finger is different but also useful, every person has his/her own special value. He/she is special, is one of a kind, and is unique. The paintbrush shape in the logo symbolizes a human palm but also color, the color that everybody needs to add in their life so as to make it more beautiful and "erase" homophobia and transphobia. It's an invitation for the public to focus on the issue and start acting.

Hand - Colours - Brush

Unity - Equality - Diversity
LGBTQ - 5 Fingers - 5 Colours

theLAB108 is a multi-shop that develops various brands from the concept of "Athleisure." The shop provides the latest trend and premium women active-wear by consistently and rapidly introducing overseas brands to women in their twenties to forties, who consider health, style, and beauty all at once. TheLAB108 seeks for the "Look and Feel" – street look which can be mixed and matched with the city look, and is not restricted to a certain space. Moreover, the look escapes the monotonous design of active-wear while maximizing femininity and securing functionality.

Design **Lee Hyojin**
Client **TheLAB108**

TheLAB108

TASK

As theLAB108 opened 3 stores in the Hyundai Department Store, the third largest store in Korea, its new "brand" started to become a necessity. Furthermore, in the current masculine and functionality-focused outdoor market, the shop tried to draw the differentiated brand strategy, which emphasizes on style and femininity. Moreover, the shop aims to provide the strong brand image of theLAB108 by a coherent design from the brand strategy and identity to the design of the brand application.

INSPIRATIONS & CONCEPTS

The brand design of theLAB108 started from the origin of "108." "1" stands for the unification of mental health and physical health based on psychological realization. "0" stands for the emptying and calming of the mind. Lastly, "8" stands for the infinite beauty. Inspired by such meanings, the brand identity was drawn as a stable column, relaxed margin, and repeating straight and curved lines. The overall communication of the brand is drawn from the motif, with the marbling expressing infinite beauty and unification of mental and physical health.

FINAL SOLUTION

The brand tone and manner are established based on the neutral tones, which are feminine gorgeous, elegant, but not excessive, implying the brand characteristics of theLAB108. The brand logo and the design essence (color, motif, typography, photography, material, and sound) are coherently applied in the overall brand application.

THE
LAB108

153

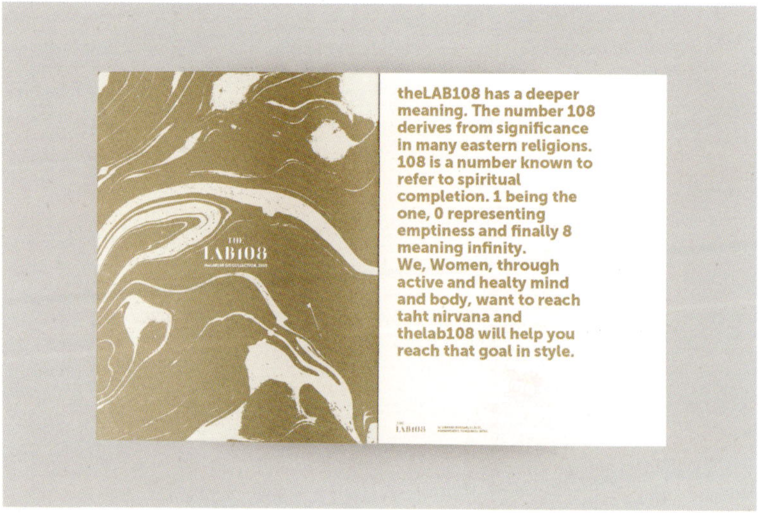

154

Sloko is an event project agency based in Saint Peterburg, Russia, specializing in corporate entertainment. The agency was found with refined and artistic personality, striving to deliver beauty and happiness to everyone's life.

Design agency **All Design Transparent**
Design **Anastasia Yakovleva, Olesia Lipskaya, Ignat Avdeev, Anton Sadovsky**
Art Direction **Anastasia Yakovleva**
Photography **Maxim Simanovich**
Client **Sloko**

Sloko

TASK
The team was commissioned to build a new brand that would be associated with the aristocratic spirit of the founder and keep a noble look through every piece of design.

INSPIRATIONS & CONCEPTS
The name Sloko is a Russian abbreviation for ivory – a commonly known symbol of wealth and well–being in India, where every day is a feast of bright colors, gold and velvet. While the team was looking for inspiration in the ivory colors and Indian culture, the outlines and curves of tusk fascinated their minds and set the right base for the logo creation.

FINAL SOLUTION
The team created a sleek and minimalistic logo which consists of the elements of type cut down to an extent (it becomes a sophisticated form, yet it remains readable). A timeless color palette, which combines cream, bronze, and navy blue was created in order to communicate the brand's name, mood, and values. They strived to comply with the brand's aesthetics and represent the features of its owner.

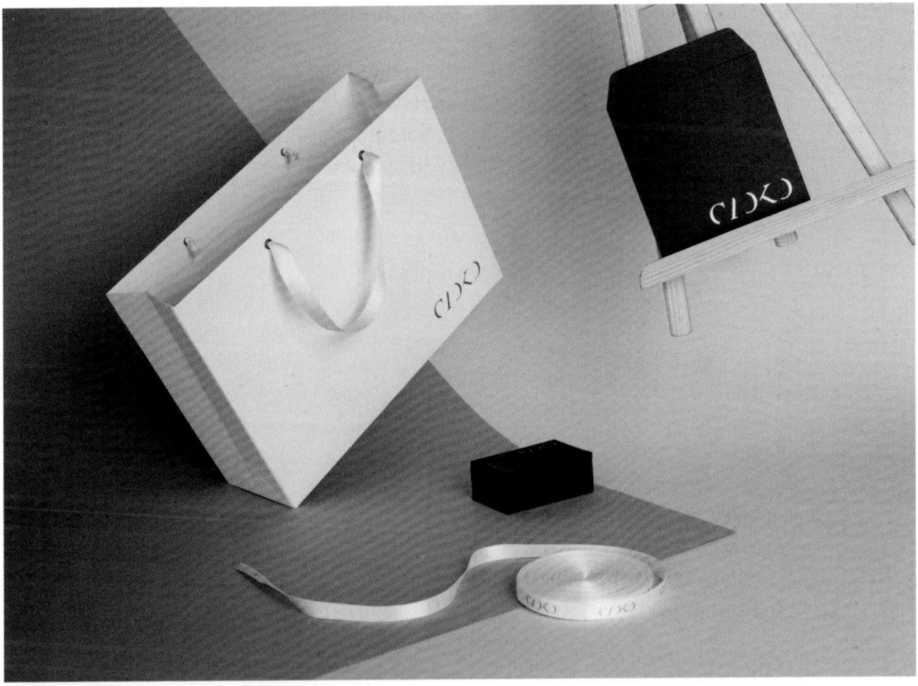

157

Brand Inteligente is an educational global platform that provides knowledge on branding, strategic design, marketing, and advertising. It is also a portal for entrepreneurs using the theme of education as a strategy to motivate, teach, and develop the skills of people, with the sole purpose that they achieve their goals.

Design **Roger Lara**
Client **Brand inteligente**

Brand Inteligente

TASK
The project was based on generating a unique brand concept according to the values of brand, a concept that should be reflected in all applications of the brand from logo level, behavior to graphics system. All parts to be developed should have a professional and amicable tone as it was a distinct feature that the brand used to stand out from other brands.

INSPIRATIONS & CONCEPTS
The team created the concept as "build inside, to create outside" as the company was dedicated to educating and generating valuable content to people. They relied on this phrase to develop the logo and other printed pieces.

FINAL SOLUTION
Under the brand concept, the logo was created with a letter "I" inside and a letter "B" outwardly. Then both letters were implemented terminations "Serif Slab" to highlight the educational and professional theme. Everything was handled in shades of black and white. The team generated a more formal and elegant character as a result.

159

La Clinique de Paris Grand Hilton Hotel Seoul has studied the anti-aging and skin care therapy program for more than 30 years and has partnered with the headquarters founded by Claude Chauchard, the specialist in the very field. It provides a new anti-aging program, skin care, body care, and spa program that are suitable for Koreans.

Design **Lee Hyojin**
Client **La Clinique de Paris Grand Hilton Seoul (Self-initiated)**

La Clinique de Paris Grand Hilton Seoul, Branding

TASK
The brand thought that renewal of the brand image was inevitable in order to provide a better communication to its customers as they had no unique brand story, tone, or manner in brand design. Furthermore, the brand strategy to carry on the main business model of anti-aging for a long-term period lacked. As one of the brands launched in the Grand Hilton Hotel Seoul, La Clinique de Paris surely needed the premium brand image strategy suitable for its prestige.

INSPIRATIONS & CONCEPTS
The brand image was derived from the keyword: "light," as it does not solely seek the physical youth but also seeks the mental health and beauty.

FINAL SOLUTION
Brand Logo: In order to visually express the consistent beauty and health sought by the brand, the light, symbolizing beauty, and the Mobius strip, symbolizing consistent and endless effort, became the motif for the brand logo. Brand Motif Pattern: The brand logo was expanded in its pattern in order to express the infinite beauty that the brand seeks for. Brand Color Palette: The color expresses a premium and sparkling image, as well as the brand's characteristics, with neutral dark brown tones that are similar with the person's skin tone. Brand Design Application: The brand aims to provide a special and coherent brand experience to its customers by applying such factors to the stationery, packaging, leaflets, interior signage, and shopping bags.

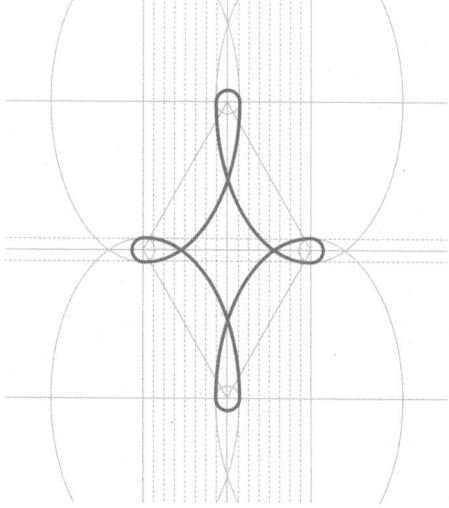

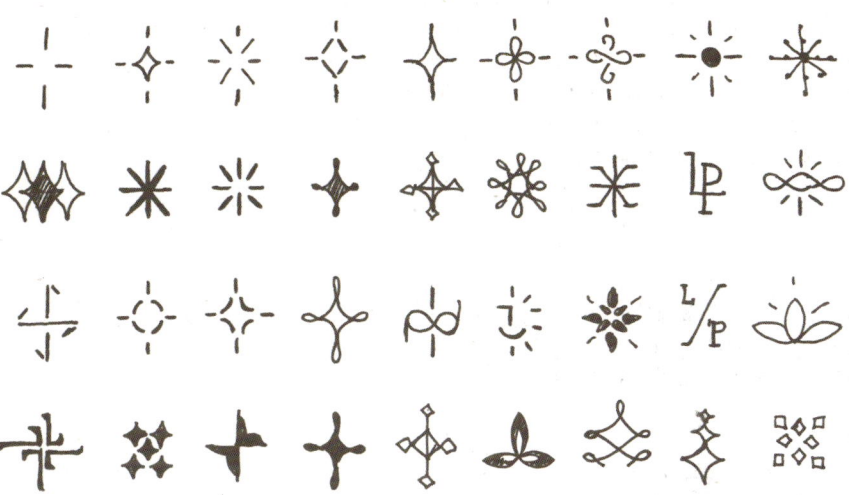

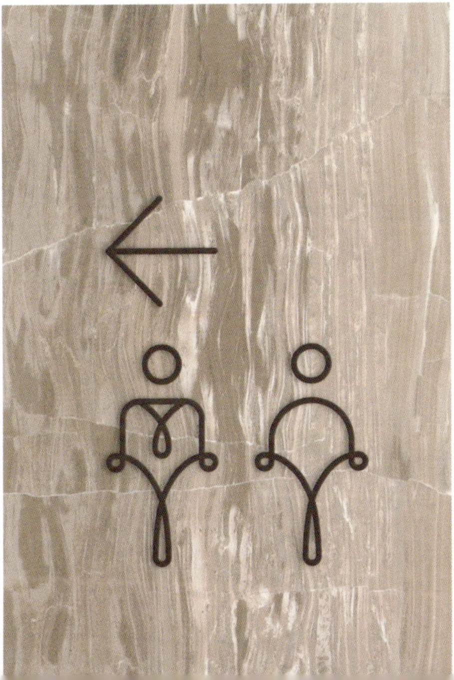

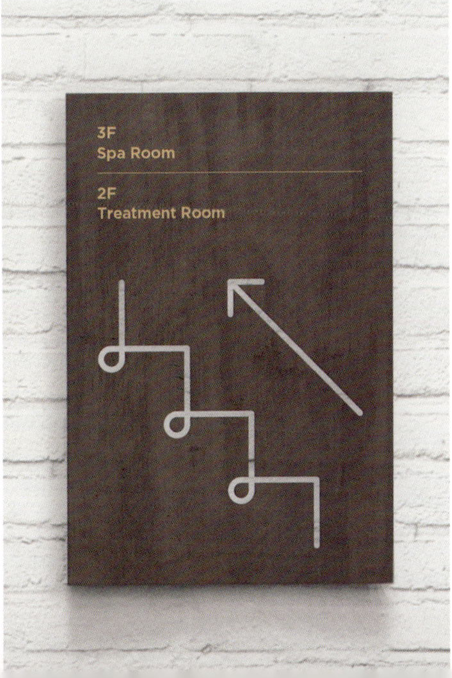

3F
Spa Room

2F
Treatment Room

Rice Moment is a creative restaurant featuring rice as its main ingredient. Rice from the east combining delicate cooking methods from the west, make experimental and exciting rice dishes.

Design agency **Transform Design**
Design **Yueh Hsin Yi**
Art direction **Huang Kuo Yu**
Client **Rice Moment**

Rice Moment

TASK
Restaurants featuring rice often give an impression of Japanese style, but Rice Moment is positioned as a western style brand with creative cooking methods. Thus the logo should express a funny, unique, and warm feeling and represent a brand new life attitude.

INSPIRATIONS & CONCEPTS
The inspiration comes from a bowl of rice, incorporating three important concepts which are rice, enjoyment, and sharing.

FINAL SOLUTION
The logo was presented with the brand's English name and looks like grains of rice from a far distance. Two words showing the sprite of the brand, "share" and "enjoy," were placed under the logo to enhance the brand's character.

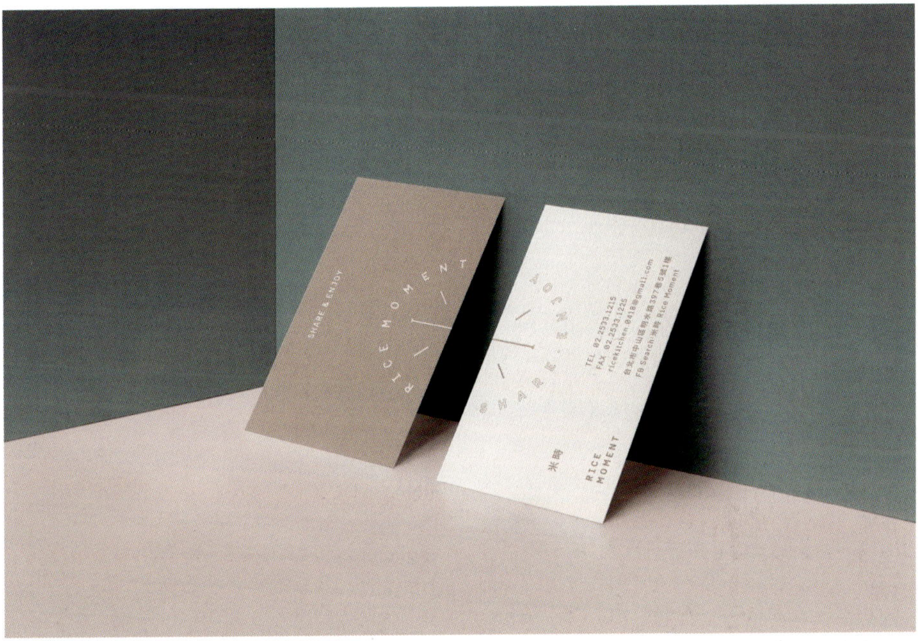

165

Huang Sheng is a flower shop with artistic character. Its name comes from the concept "born from flower." It provides proper flower design for festivals and its client's special occasions.

Design agency **Transform Design**
Design **Szu Ling Shen**
Art direction **Huang Kuo Yu**
Client **Hua Sheng Flora Design**

Hua Sheng Floral Design

TASK
As there are many flower shops in the market, the brand visual of Hua Sheng needed to reflect that it's both professional and artistic so as to stand out from its competitors. Thus the team chose a rather abstract and modern way to create the visual identity.

INSPIRATIONS & CONCEPTS
To the design team, flower is the best symbol to represent the connections between people, and the design must transfer the warmness of the connection to the audience.

FINAL SOLUTION
The two letters "H" and "S," initials of "Hua Sheng," were intertwined and connected like clusters of flowers. Photos of flowers were abstracted and patterned as supporting visuals to give a unique artistic feeling.

Condes de Albarei is an internationally recognized winery based in Galicia, north of Spain, that markets white wine under Albariño variety since 1988. Throughout their long history, Condes de Albarei has won several international awards and recognitions.

Design **Lucas Gil-Turner**
Client **Adega Condes de Albarei**

Condes de Albarei

TASK
Condes de Albarei contacted the team to submit a proposal with the intention to reposition their brand through the design of a new visual identity, conveying values and essence of the winery through a simple, recognizable, and functional language.

INSPIRATIONS & CONCEPTS
For the proposal, the team sought the inspiration in the curves and circular shapes that exist around the wine (grape, bottle, sea, glass, etc.). They tried to capture the impact of a drop when it falls into liquid and the waves generated around. From here they designed a symbol with five circles in constant growth and rotation – representing the process and evolution of the harvest.

FINAL SOLUTION
The proposal was based on a symbol that reflects the values of the brand through a simple and modern language. Through a comprehensive color range, different sub-brands were presented but the whole product supply was unified under a single brand.

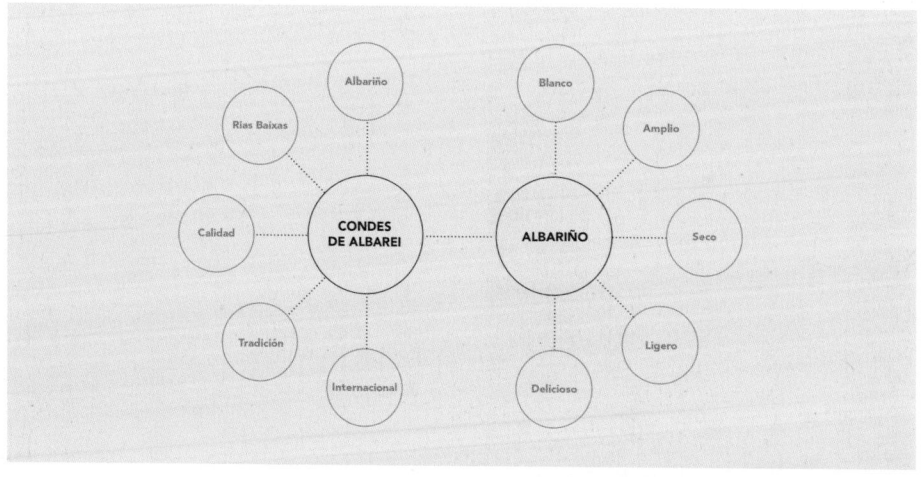

Brand architecture

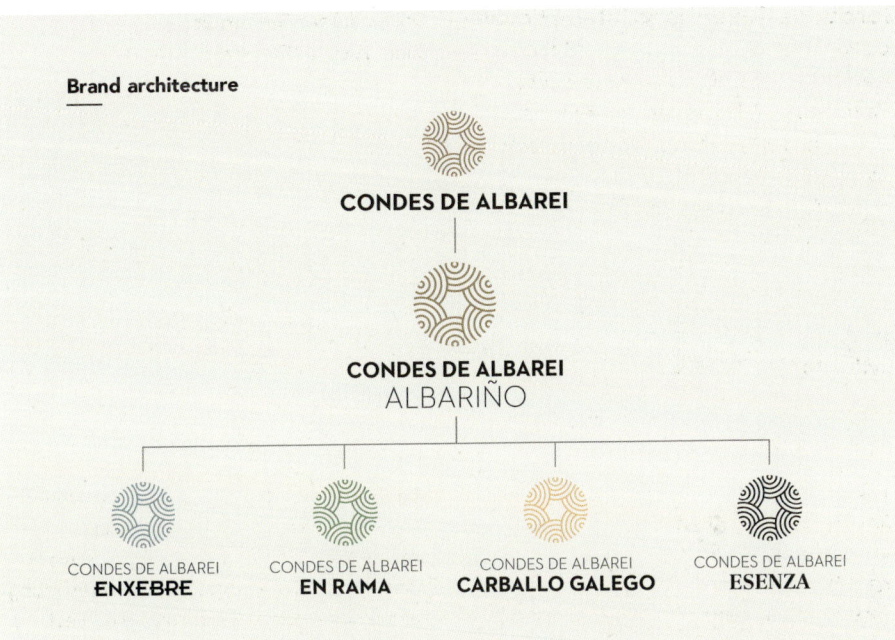

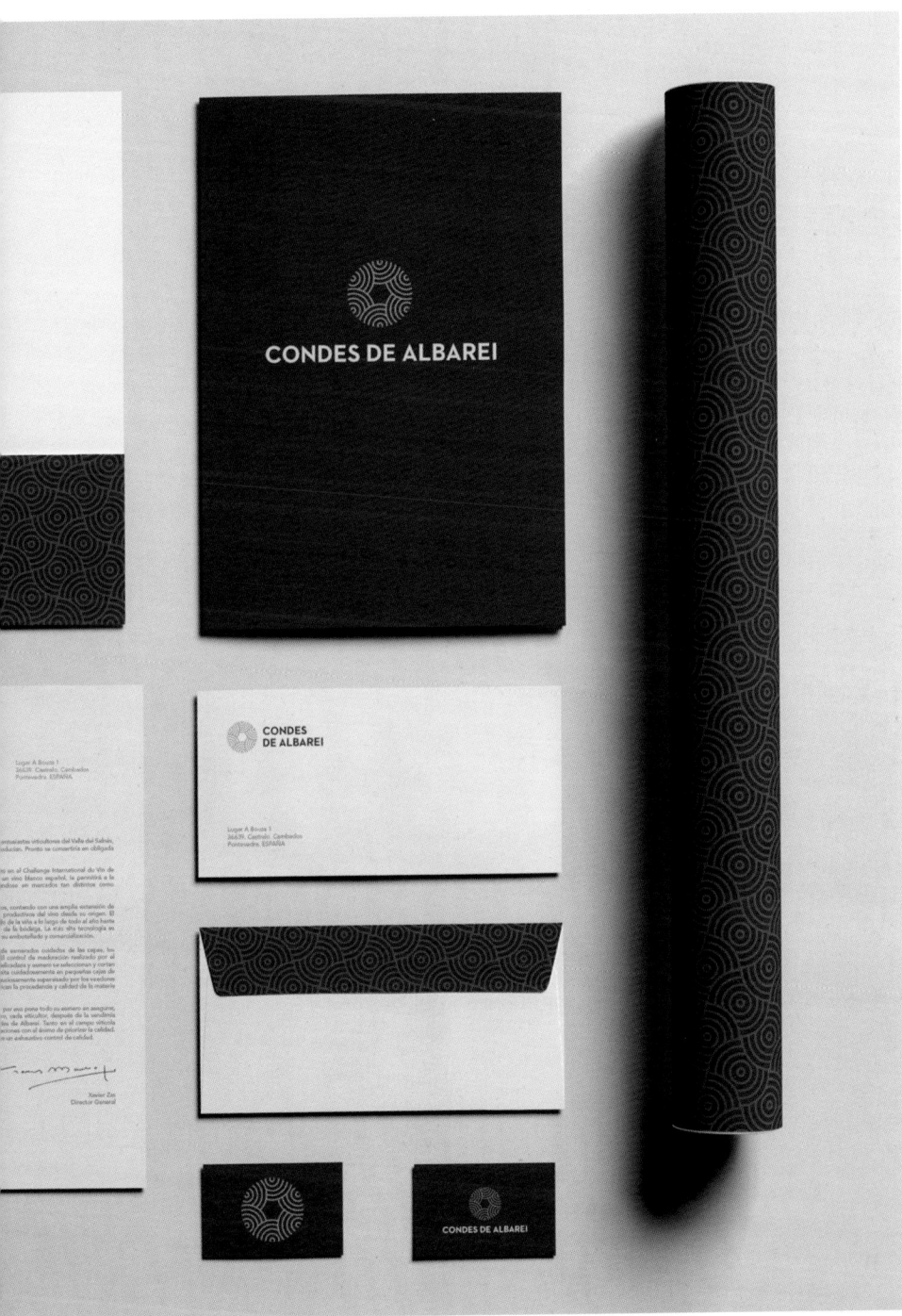

After graduating in graphic design at IESB – Educational Institution of Brasília (Instituto de Educação de Brasília), the designer found there was a necessity of a personal brand. It was challenging to create his own brand so he could start his career as a fresh new designer. Through the research process and benchmark he analyzed the best way to create the identity that could pass the message of what was truly important, within his aspects as a designer, and in the construction of the concept of a brand.

Design **Henrique Dias**
Photography **Ricardo Monserratt**
Client **Henrique Dias**

Henrique Dias Personal Branding

TASK
The mission was to communicate the quality and sophistication with which the designer applies in his projects. Once the elements which permeate the identity were created, the process of creating the graphic pieces began.

INSPIRATIONS & CONCEPTS
The brand was designed to be clear, consistent, and objective. It is a simple visual identity, with a symmetric symbol derived from geometric forms. The brand was inspired by the symbolism of focus and the perception of a target, on which the designer based his design. The contrast between the colors was designed to give the viewers a feeling of seriousness (by the navy blue) and provocation of perception (by the red). providing a great composition for the brand.

FINAL SOLUTION
The main aesthetic of the logo is the monogram of an H within a square. A simple form where the letter to be placed as negative space has given many forms and patterns when multiplied, like a snow flake or a target, with symmetrical symbols.

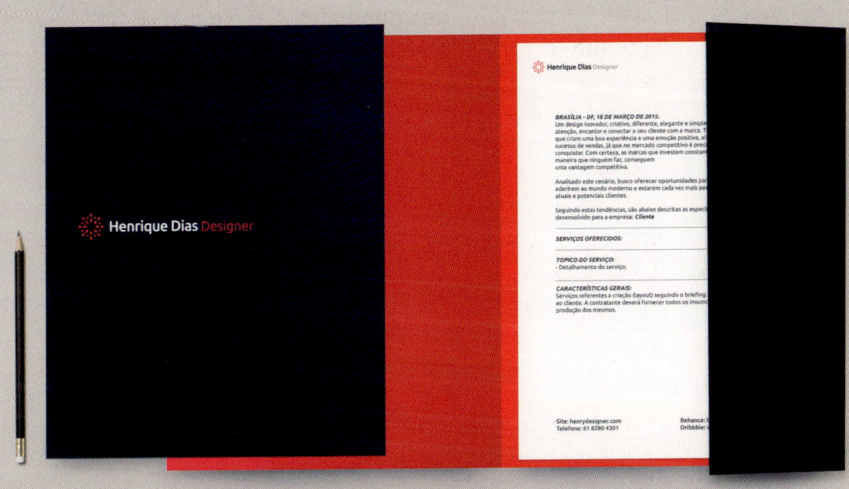

173

The Assembly Store is a multi-label men's fashion store that provides consumers a consistent and carefully curated array of merchandise, a one-stop-shop that offers the conceptual selection of clothing, accessories, and collectibles. It presents a lifestyle experience for the fun and spontaneous gentlemen who appreciate quality. Alongside the retail arm, The Assembly Ground is a casual cafe, offering a respite for their consumers to rest, exchange ideas and experiences, or just to hang out.

The Assembly

TASK
The task was to create an identity for the store that doesn't represent any direct label but reflects the lifestyle of its customers.

INSPIRATIONS & CONCEPTS
The main concept was to create a space where like-minded individuals gather to appreciate a shared lifestyle that the Assembly provides.

FINAL SOLUTION
The identity that the team has crafted for the Assembly is classic, versatile, and playful. The logomark is a styled version of a base of a campfire to represent the idea of the store and cafe as places of convocation. The Assembly's color palette is highly saturated to bring life to the brand, whilst a graphic system that consists of classic fabric patterns reflects the gentlemen style.

Design agency **Bravo**
Creative director **Edwin Tan**
Design **Jasmine Lee**
Project management **Janice Teo**
Client **Benjamin Barker**

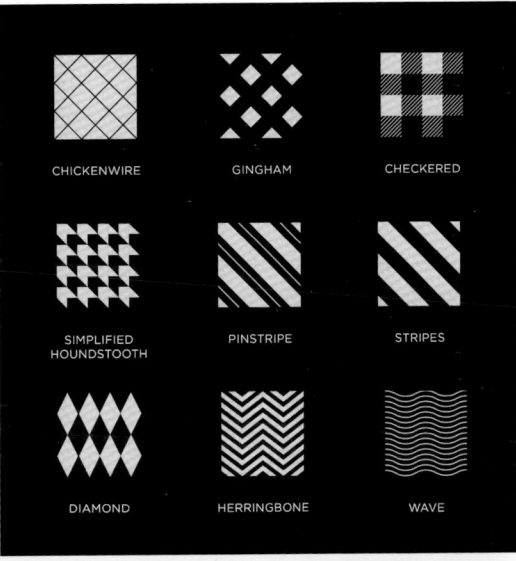

303 Design Squadron is a design studio based in Porto Alegre, Brazil, formed by a multidisciplinary and well experienced team of designers, specialized in branding and visual communication.

Design **303 Design Squadron**
Creative direction **Henrique Braga, Tiago Berao, Gustavo Andrighetto**
Client **303 Design Squadron**

303 Design Squadron

TASK
The task was to develop a meaningful and memorable branding concept for the team's own design studio that translates their skills and vision of design and to inspire and build confidence to their clients.

INSPIRATIONS & CONCEPTS
In the autumn of 1940, during the Second World War, a group of well experienced and talented polish pilots who voluntarily served the Royal Air Force (RAF) for the Battle of Britain formed what turned out to be their best and most effective squad, the 303 Polish Fighter Squadron. Facing this historical context and a few coincidences, like the number of their first studio was 303, the team has decided to metaphorically incorporate the name for 303 Design Squadron.

FINAL SOLUTION
In order to create a connection to the historical context, the team developed an illustration of a Hawker Hurricane Mk I, aircraft used by the squadron at the Second World War. To compose the visual signature they created a minimalism and modern logotype for the number 303, which serves as the base aesthetic for all stationery set, generating a more sophisticated and elegant look.

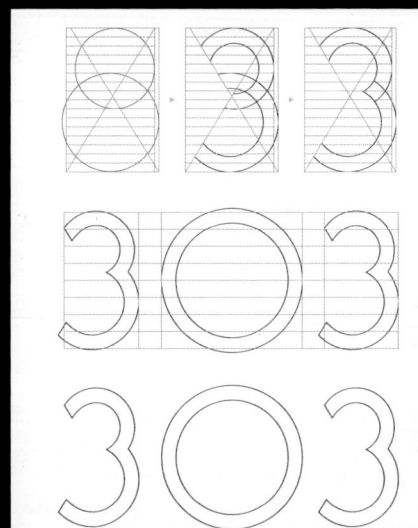

303
HENRIQUEBRAGA
+ 55 51 3095.2289
+ 55 51 9744.9582
HENRIQUE@303DESIGN.COM.BR
WWW.303DESIGN.COM.BR
303 DESIGN SQUADRON
303
TIAGOBERAO
+ 55 51 3095.2289
+ 55 51 9121.3900
TIAGO@303DESIGN.COM.BR
WWW.303DESIGN.COM.BR
303 DESIGN SQUADRON

303 DESIGN SQUADRON
303 DESIGN SQUADRON
3. March. 2014 - POA

Ninja Interns was a winner team in an internship competition held in 2015. The main aim of the competition was to learn and practice web design while working on 7 un-commercial social projects.

Design **Andriy Yurchenko, Olena Postoi, Diana Askerova, Olexandra Sudak, Anastasia Teslenko, Valentina Milashevska**
Client **Alexander Tregub**

Ninja Interns

TASK
In this project the task was to create a team name and its identity.

INSPIRATIONS & CONCEPTS
The team decided that ninja was a good idea to name the team. It's a very interesting character because of its history and meaning.

Good ninjas are multifunctional fighters and work imperceptibly.

FINAL SOLUTION
Finally the team got a very good team name, logo, and brand identity. In the logo 3 hidden meanings can be found. The logo also interacts well with pattern.

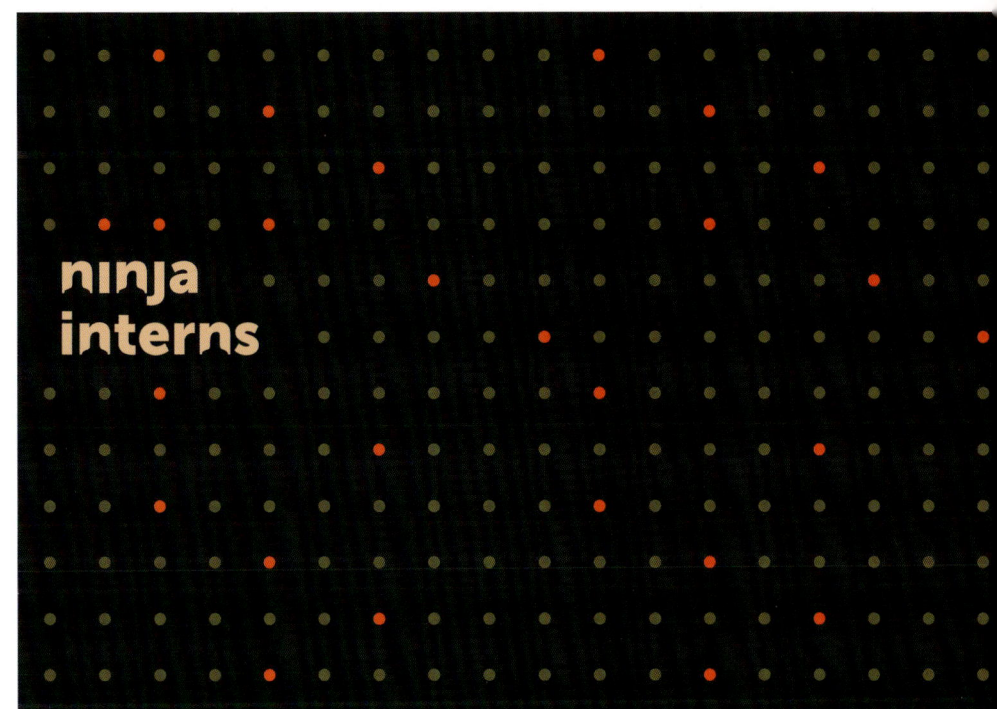

ninja
interns
Andriy Yurchenko
daimyo ninja

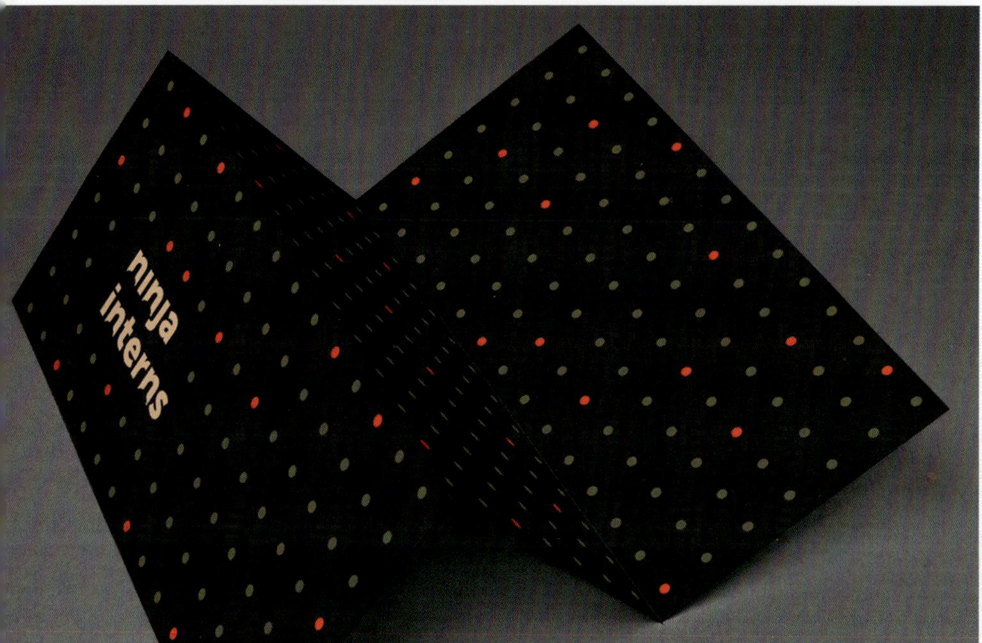
ninja
interns

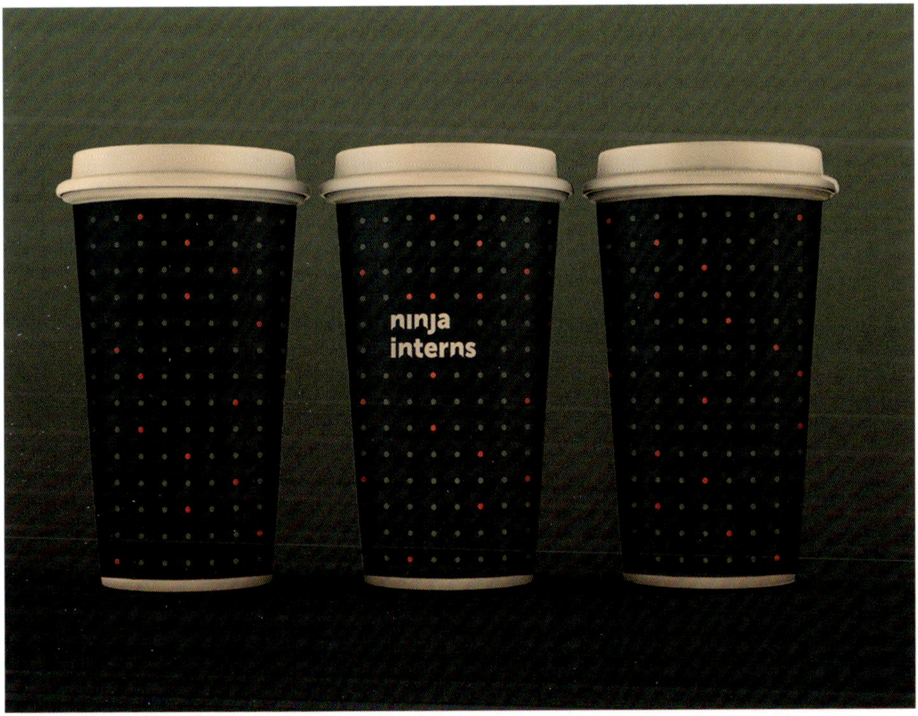
ninja
interns

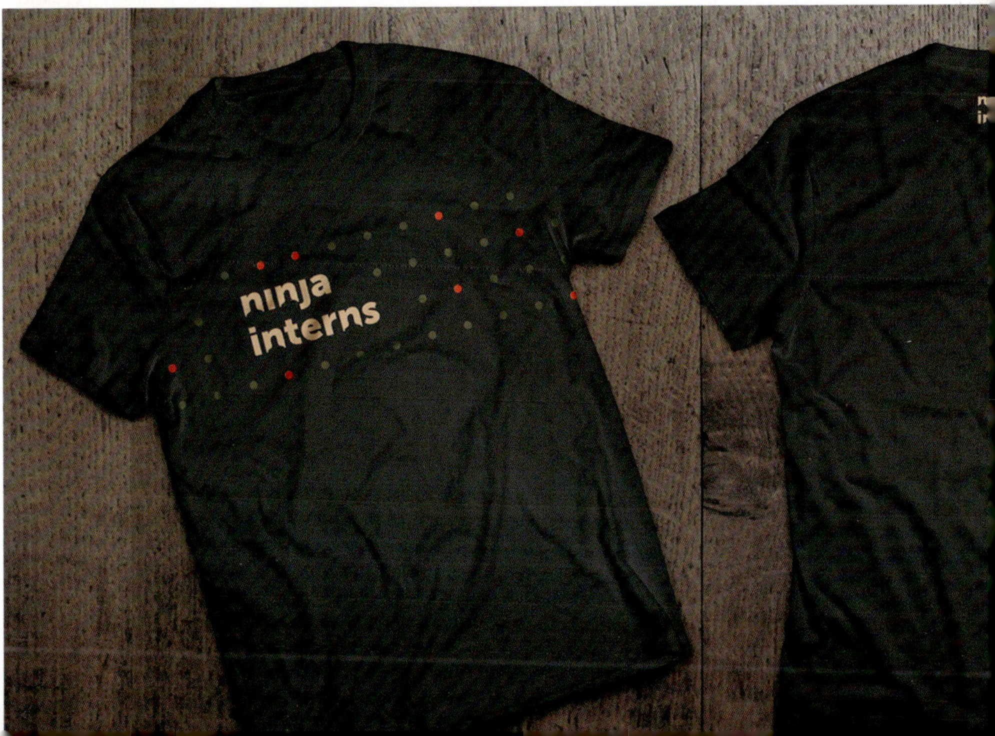
ninja
interns

The NUVO furniture company was established in 1989 in Ballito, South Africa and celebrated its 25th anniversary in 2014. NUVO only utilizes the latest equipment for the production of their steel based furniture. Considering the design of the pieces NUVO is offering a very unique look and simple style, following the global trend of reduced design.

Design **Felix Kraus**
Client **NUVO Furniture**

NUVO

TASK
As the company was celebrating its 25th anniversary in 2014 and considering an exploration of the online market as a new way of doing business, rebranding was needed. The target customers were young people in their 25-35 years old, who are successful in their career and know how to appreciate design furniture. They are often well educated and used to online shopping. To meet the needs of the target customers, the essence of the rebrand must be modern, artificial, and have a quality of simplicity.

INSPIRATIONS & CONCEPTS
"Creating and finding spaces where you won't have guessed" is the credo of NUVO. NUVO is all about creating spaces and that is also the main design technique used. The concept finds its place in the logo and also in the rest of the design. Creating large negative white areas that arouse tension and highlight indirectly given information contribute to the design for the company.

FINAL SOLUTION
The result was based on a scamp as simple as it could get – the company name in a box that symbolizes the very basic of NUVO's furniture style. Adding a third dimension creates

(fictional) space which perfectly reflects NUVO's way of always trying to create new spaces for their customers. Going even further with this point, the designer generated a fluid design which can be arranged in a given grid – similar to the arrangement of furniture in a room which varies from time to time.

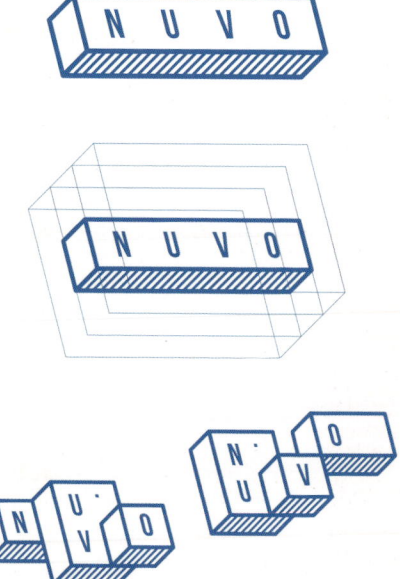

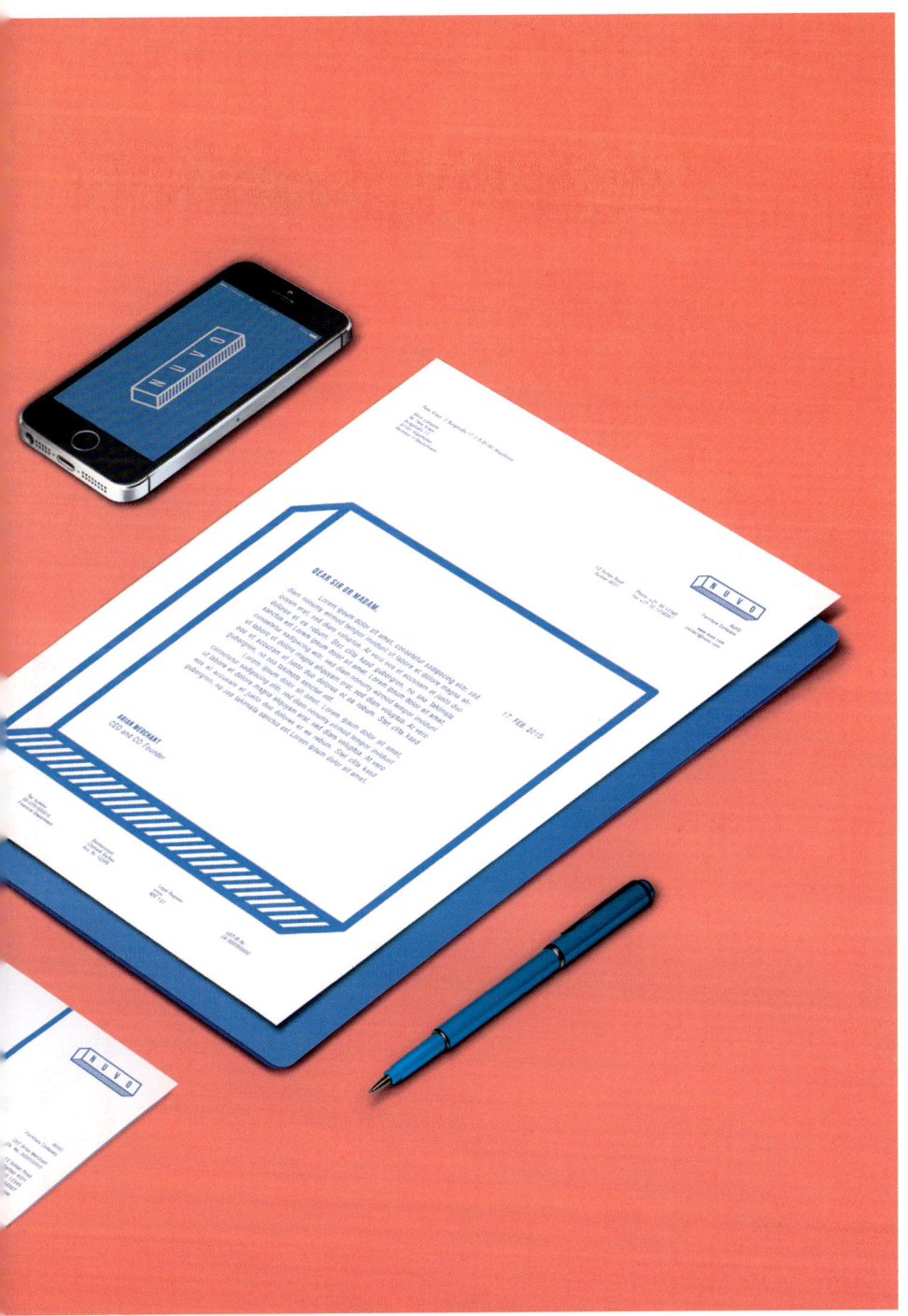

LINEUP is a surf apparel brand residing in the United States of America.

Design **Chris Edwards**
Client **LINEUP Apparel**

LINEUP Surf Apparel

TASK
The nature of this brand was to be styled minimally, which led to a process of producing a bold yet simple logo using the waves of the ocean as an important element.

INSPIRATIONS & CONCEPTS
The designer was inspired by the waves of the ocean, which were brought together through a minimal aesthetic. The abstract direction accompanied with an equally fitting typeface contrasted an effective result to demonstrate the closer relation to the company's coastal culture.

FINAL SOLUTION
The final solution retained the form of the logo. The designer paid key attention to scale to make the text and the icon work in harmony with each other. To extend the uses of the logo, the designer played with the logo's application, which led to unofficial merchandise concepts for bags, t-shirts, and print products.

191

Hidden District is a project that started in Brussels when a group of friends began to meet to discuss a range of cultural and social issues over dinners. They took turns in hosting the events. Participants found it a great way to switch off from the daily routine as well as a fun way to meet people. They found the experience so enriching that they were convinced that it would appeal to many others. So they decided to open it up to the public and share it with others who would contribute something of their own.

Hidden District

TASK
As the project continued to grow, it became clear that it required a brand and a marketing strategy. Since good food and drink had always been a basic part of the experience, the founders thought it might be a good idea to market a range of wines under a single brand. It was at that point that they contacted Mimética to assist them in the brand creation process, from the initial idea, through the choice of a name, to the packaging for the wine.

INSPIRATIONS & CONCEPTS
Hidden District, is a fantasy land right there where people live, a neverland where people can be a kid again. It is the reward awaiting curious urban explorers with the ability to look at their surroundings with new eyes. It is a refuge from the daily grind of urban life, a respite from the boring exchanges of the workplace, and a place where people can freely discuss the issues that really matter to them while enjoying good food and wine.

FINAL SOLUTION
Starting from this idea, the team developed the identity. The logo is a diagram of an urban layout. In a play on the idea of the city's hidden spaces, "Hidden" hides behind "District" in the logo. The team found the inspiration in the urban and subway maps and used the Transat font in the texts but made the letters of the logo from scratch to place it in the map grid. They didn't use specific colors in the logo because the idea was to change the colors in each new batch of wine.

Design agency **Mimética**
Design **Javier Montañés**
Photography **Luis Sainz**
Client **Hidden District**

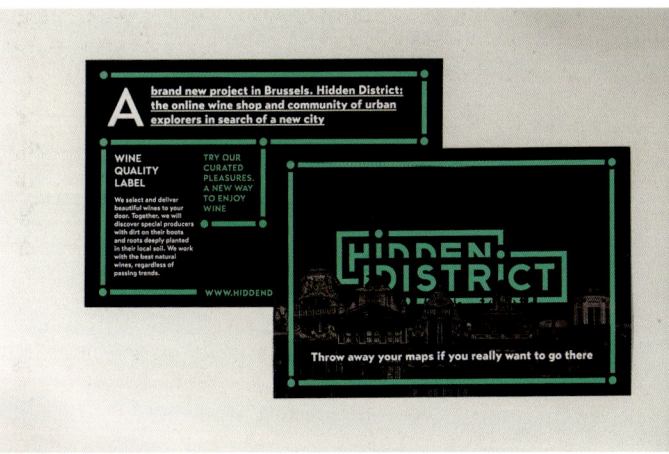

The Saastamoinen Foundation Art Collection is one of the most significant private collections in Finland. The central role of the foundation is to develop and showcase its collection consisting of 2,500 works.

Design agency **Kuudes Kerros**
Design **Tony Eräpuro**
Photography **Paavo Lehtonen**
Client **Saastamoinen Foundation**

Saastamoinen Foundation

TASK
Although founded in 1968, the foundation lacked a visual identity. The Saastamoinen Foundation is an international expert and influencer within the fields of science, culture, and art. Thus a VI reflecting its character must be created.

INSPIRATIONS & CONCEPTS
The team designed a visual identity that enhances its international, contemporary image and its powerful devotion to lead the society further. The identity was inspired by the golden ratio, a divine proportion that is broadly manifested in art, science, architecture, music, and the nature.

FINAL SOLUTION
Amidst the black and white identity is a transforming logo that traces the golden ratio. The letters in the logo are not fixed: they can randomly switch places and form abstract combinations. The logo works especially well in animations, where it forms different letter combinations that change infinitely.

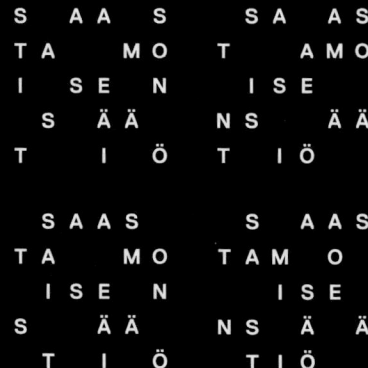

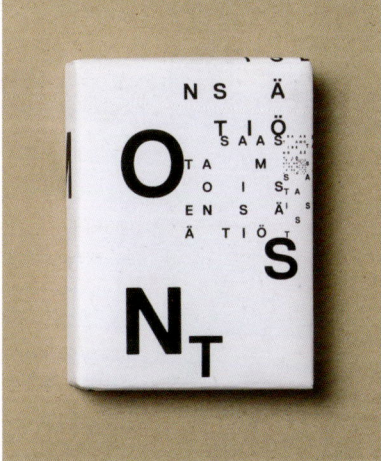

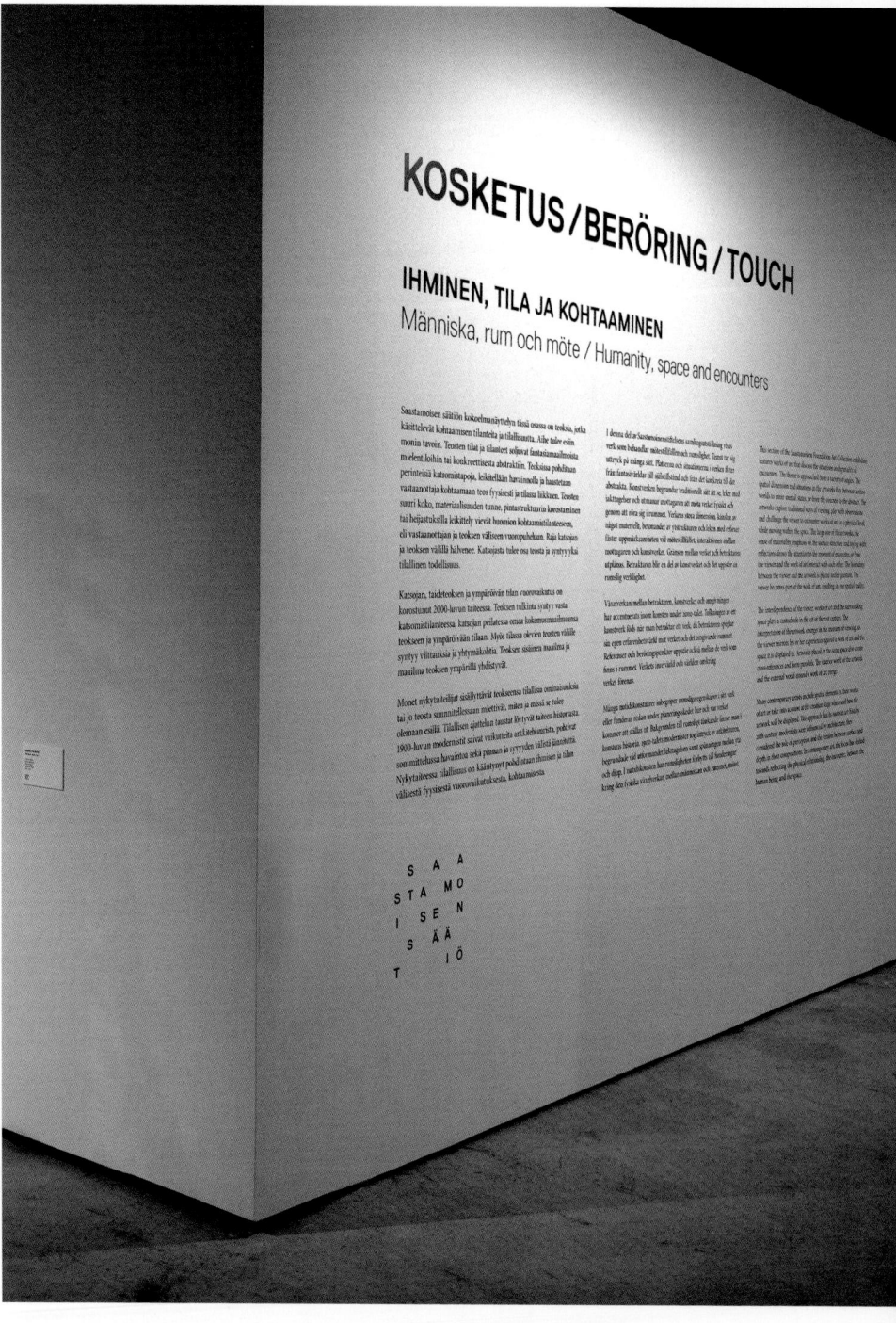

Ut: Studentbyrå is a creative agency by and for students in the creative industry in Norway. The project was initiated by creative agency Superblaise with the idea of giving the students valuable experience working with real briefs and interdisciplinary teamwork, and an opportunity to show their talent to potential clients and employers.

Design **Mads Sæløen**
Client **Superblaise AS**

Ut: Studentbyrå

TASK
Develop a concept and visual identity for a creative agency for and by students.

INSPIRATIONS & CONCEPTS
The team found the inspiration for the concept "Ut: Studentbyrå" in one of their initial ideas called "Ut av redet Studentbyrå," which loosely translates to "out of the nest student agency." After long discussions the team realized that "Ut" is the start of many different words in the Norwegian language, including "Utforske(Explore)," "Utfordre(Challenge)," and "Utvikle(Develop)." All these made the name "Ut:" a very good fit, as it could be built upon and extended in the future.

FINAL SOLUTION
The final logomark is a combination of the letters U, T, and a semicolon, leaving room for expansion while stating the goal of the agency – that the students are heading out into the professional, creative industry.

Talkin' Threads – Limited Edition, a fashion and high street brand. The UPS (unique selling point) of the brand is using design tools like drawing, spray painting, mist, and rapid fire graffiti tools to attract its target audience who are young hip design and fashion savvy adults between 14-30.

Design **Maurizio Pagnozzi**
Client **Talkin' Threads**

Talkin' Threads – Limited Edition

TASK
The brand should be intriguing to use as a product, for example used on T-shirts and on other articles produced. During the briefing the team asked the client: "Are there any specific images or icons you'd like to incorporate into the logo?" The client responded: "Any elements or icons you feel fit the brand and our needs. We need young adults to think this is 'sick,' want to wear it, or will recognize it immediately."

INSPIRATIONS & CONCEPTS
The shape of the logo has been designed to be clean and straightforward. The main purpose was to go directly to the core. The concept was to combine three elements: the monogram of the initials of the name (TT for Talkin' Threads), the pedestrian crossing, as a reference to the street, and the rude gesture middle finger to make the logo really memorable in the minds of consumers.

FINAL SOLUTION
The logo is colored black, but it can change color depending on the purpose (on T-shirts, sweatshirts, or other clothings). An example is the pattern created for the edition of the packaging of the gift card. The font chosen is a linear sans serif, with a modern and up-to-date character, little rounded in order to make the viewers remember the lines of the logo.

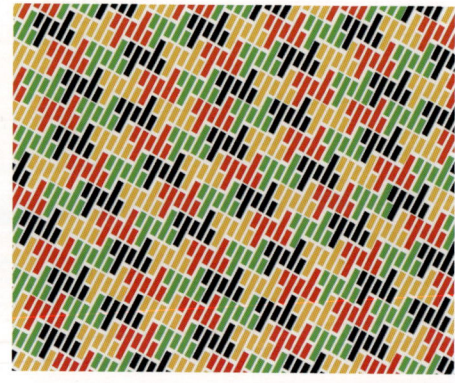

203

NoizeFilms is a corporate movie production company based in São Paulo, Brazil. It was founded to meet a market demand for high quality corporate videos, since there were no such companies focused only on doing this.

Design agency **Lud/co. Studio**
Design **Renan Artur Vizzotto**
Client **NoizeFilms**

NoizeFilms

TASK
The client asked the team to create a modern and clean logo that could position NoizeFilms as a unique video production company which is attentive to details. The team needed to develop a visual identity that transmitted NoizeFilms' team spirit and showed the company's unique thinking.

INSPIRATIONS & CONCEPTS
To attend the client's request for a really intelligent and dynamic logo, the team went looking for references and elements in movie classics, the roots of motion pictures productions, photography, painting, and camera mechanics and functionality, until they found their main inspiration: the human vision. The human eyes work as a camera, capturing the image in reverse. Then, when the image reaches the back part of the eye, it's processed and reversed so we can understand what we are seeing.

FINAL SOLUTION
Since the team understood the mechanics of the human eye and its resemblance to the camera functionality, they moved on to the stage of the logo development. The two lines that cross each other represent the imaginary line of the eye capturing the image. These crossed lines also represent the widely known expression "cut," used in the movie business. The team also created a pattern with the symbol, representing a constructive mesh, like a regenerating tissue. The geometric type was chosen to match the symbol, which is also extremely geometric. The golden color was used to bring a classic feel, like the golden age of big movie productions. The black color goes in as a sober color, necessary to show the serious side of NoizeFilms.

Blowhammer (BH) is a clothing brand which emphasizes the Italian underground style, blending the variety of international design and the quality of raw materials completely treated in Italy. It is the manifesto of young people who break the rules.

BH clothes express the pride about thinking using your own mind and the enthusiasm to belong to a group of people who know what they want. Blowhammer is the symbol for those who want to speak differently to the world.

Blowhammer

Task
The designer was assigned in 2015 to create a logo for Blowhhammer to represent its street-savvy style, high-quality products, and the spirit of the brand.

Inspirations & concepts
The ultimate goal of the rebranding was to create a mark that could be memorable, wearable, and suitable for possible future expansion of the brand, and could be applied on accessories, brooches, and other possible products.

Final solution
The logo is constructed from a triangle. The monogram BH can be apparently read, but if you heed it you will find out the triangle contains all the letters of the word "Blowhammer." The pattern was built along the lines of the various letters. The institutional color of the brand is black, the color that best expresses the spirit of a "sophisticated" street brand.

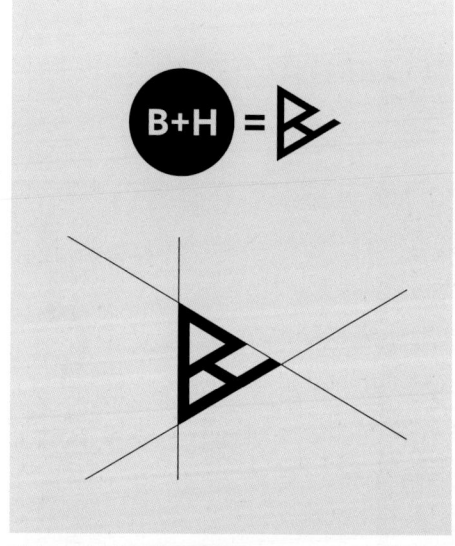

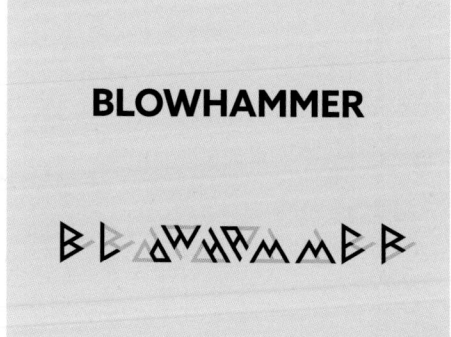

Design **Maurizio Pagnozzi**
Client **Blowhammer**

March is a collaboration of architects and creative marketing professionals founded in 1998 in Santa Monica by two partners. The partnership offers experience and innovation in marketing, strategy, and design. The core mission of March is to build brand value through architecture.

Design **Zivan Rosic**
Client **March Flux Branding**

March

TASK
The task was to create several logos and visual system directions that would aid in creating a new cohesive brand identity after renaming March.

INSPIRATIONS & CONCEPTS
The word March evokes powerful emotions, both as a month in the calendar associated with spring and renewal and as an act. The word itself is foundational in creating visuals that would complement it. The studio's ethos of placing clients' needs over architectural style allowed for the concept of "transparency" (used in a thank you card) in the visual system.

FINAL SOLUTION
The logomark is an "M," minimal and stylized to evoke architectural forms and hint at the act of "marching" (placing one leg strait in front of the other). A sober gray and black color palette was chosen to mirror primary palettes of architectural forms, along with accented bright colors picked by the partners. Helvetica Neue was chosen as logotype for its neutral qualities and balance with the mark. Lastly, the dot grid was meant to evoke both an overhead view of a "march," and architectural grids.

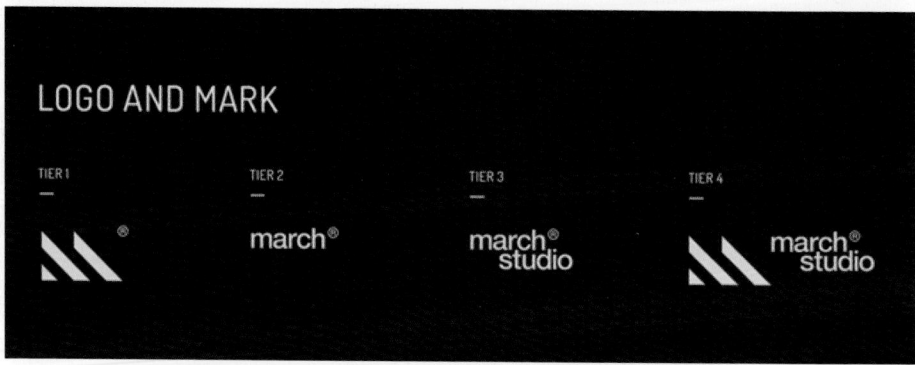

¿Qué tal? Films is a production company based in Florianópolis, SC, Brazil. Its founders come from different, yet very close countries: one is from Argentina and the other from Brazil. Its expertise is shooting all sorts of videos, like clips, commercials, and short and feature films in its own and unique way. Proof of its competence is that in only a few months' existence, it has been awarded for a short film.

Design agency **Lud/co. Studio**
Design **Renan Artur Vizzotto, Thiago Soares**
Creative direction **Caio Evangelista**
Client **¿Qué tal? Films**

¿Qué tal?

TASK
The first task was to create a name transmitting the Argentine identity, which is highly valued in Brazil for its well-known sensitivity in movie direction. The second was to balance both nationalities, making the Brazilian side noticeable. The main goal was to create a remarkable and fresh logo that could transmit what the brand was for and where it came from.

INSPIRATIONS & CONCEPTS
To start the brainstorm for the naming part, the designers teamed up with the copywriter, immersing in the Spanish language universe, searching and getting to know daily expressions used in Argentina and Brazil. The goal was to find something common in both countries and easy to say. For the logo and visual identity, the team went to look for movie production elements and icons, trying to avoid the obvious ones, like the movie roll or cameras.

FINAL SOLUTION
The solution for the name emerged from the highly known expression "¿qué tal?," which in English means "what's up?." Since the name was very porteño, the visual identity should pend a little to the Brazilian side to balance it up. For the brand, the solution was inspired by the iconic director's chair, formed minimally by two simple shapes. Also, the rectangular shape resembles a movie screen, having the same exact proportion. The main color chosen was yellow, combined with a dark blue. Both yellow and blue are in Brazil's and Argentina's national flags (in different shades). The font (Swiss 721) is a modern type, matching the geometric lines from the visual identity.

brand
¿qué tal? films
book
Brandbook

Helon Borba
helon@quetalfilms.com
55 48 3445.2125
www.quetalfilms.com

Adventure Films is a creativity-led independent film production company based in Luxembourg. The company creates a real mix of film pieces from contemporary TV commercials to corporate films for businesses across Belgium and Luxembourg. They are visual storytellers.

Design agency **Studio Lane**
Design **Sam Lane**
Client **Adventure Films**

Adventure Films

TASK
The task was to create a clean identity that matched the name of the company and stood out against competitors in the marketplace.

INSPIRATIONS & CONCEPTS
The team took inspiration from industrial materials to create a unique look and feel that stood out in the film sector. To reinforce the Industrial look and feel of the brand, unique screw, post binding, and die cuts were used throughout the print materials. This comes to life most prominently in the unique die cut business cards.

FINAL SOLUTION
The team created a custom stencil-like rounded logo, which is unique to the Adventure brand. It has strong Industrial references but with a much more rounded friendlier craft and feel to represent the ethos and structure of the company. The team wanted the brand to have a playful touch whilst at the same time have a hard, professional edge.

The team used primarily one color that the brand could own and be recognised for. They chose orange as it is a bold, warm, and friendly color without being too overpowering or aggressive. The color also complimented the rounded shapes of the logo and letterforms and worked with the core color palette of black and white. Arial Rounded was used as the primary font as it complimented the formation of the logo and reinforced that playful identity of the brand.

To show the "storytelling" qualities of the brand, the copy has been carefully crafted to help bring the warm and friendly nature of the company across. Quotes have been hand-picked from iconic films to help represent the idea of taking clients to an exciting adventure.

212

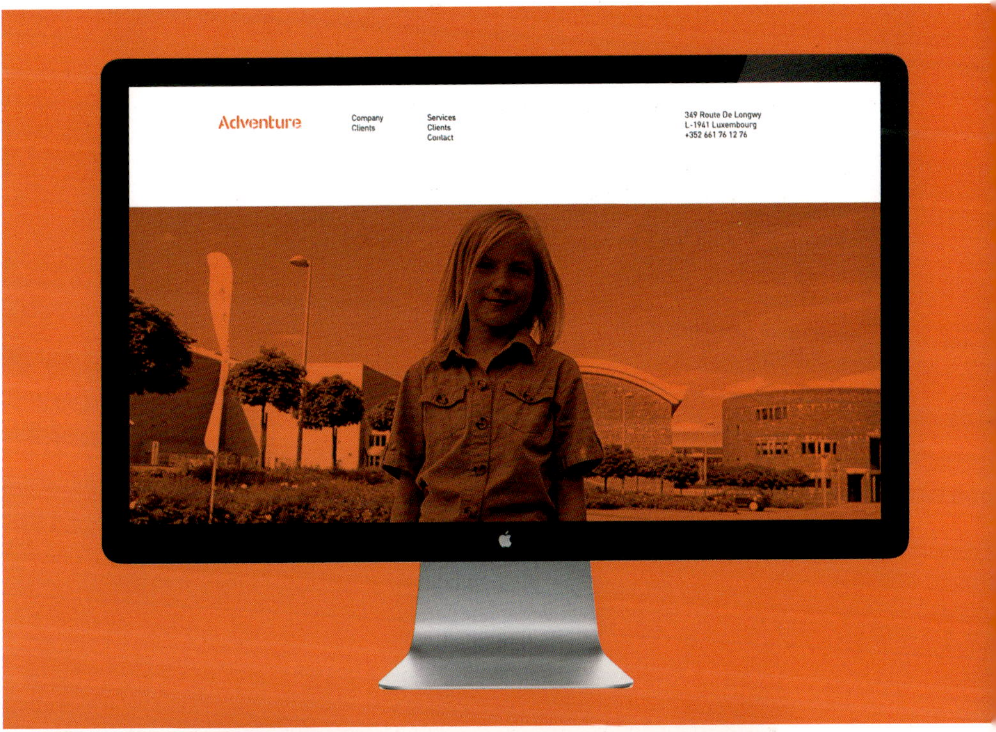

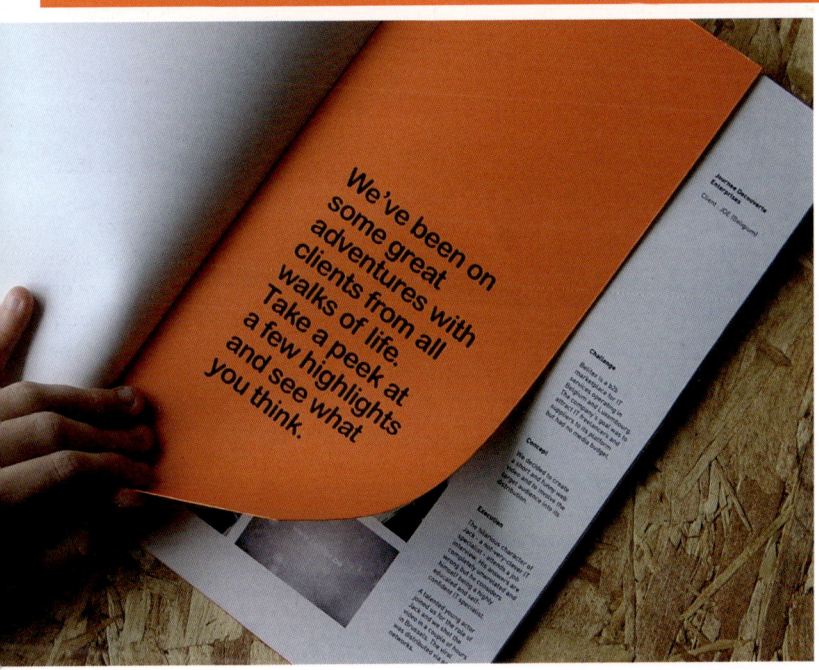

213

Studio Symphonico is a community that uses sound as its main element in the process of creative communication.

Design **Ohimena Studio**
Art direction **Luigi Durante, Silvia Pisani**
Client **Studio Symphonico**

Studio Symphonico

TASK
The tasks included company naming, logo creation, corporate identity design, and web design.

INSPIRATIONS & CONCEPTS
The answer to the search for a new identity gave a new name to the logo, which was contextualized to sound language. The logo becomes a symbol of the break crotchet duplicated, creating a distorted element.

FINAL SOLUTION
Distorted as musical process, the sound wave altered ad hoc becomes the underlying theme of the corporate identity.

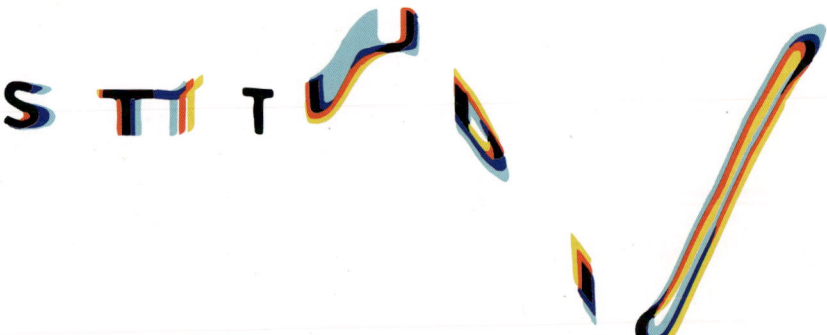

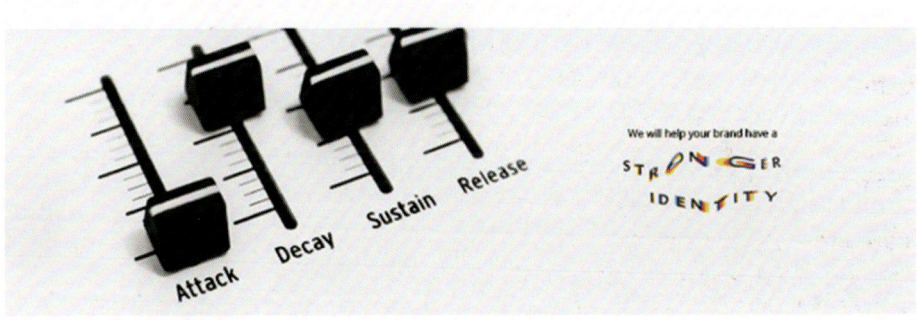

SELECTED WORKS

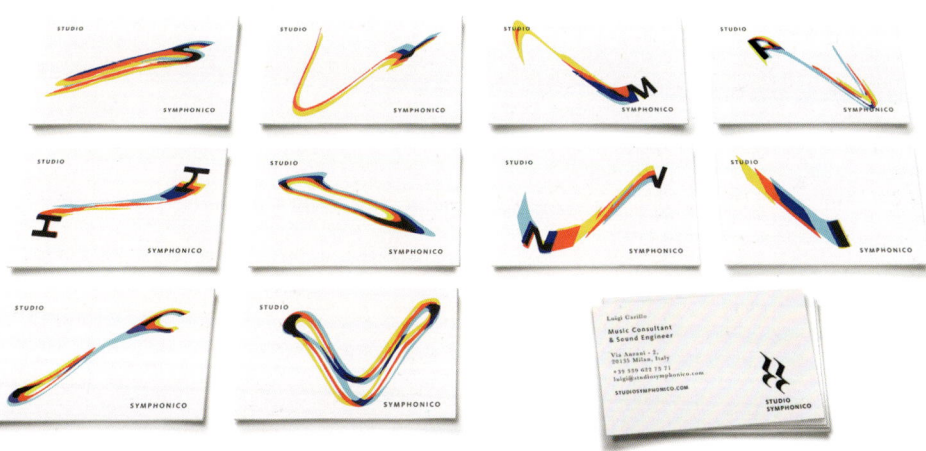

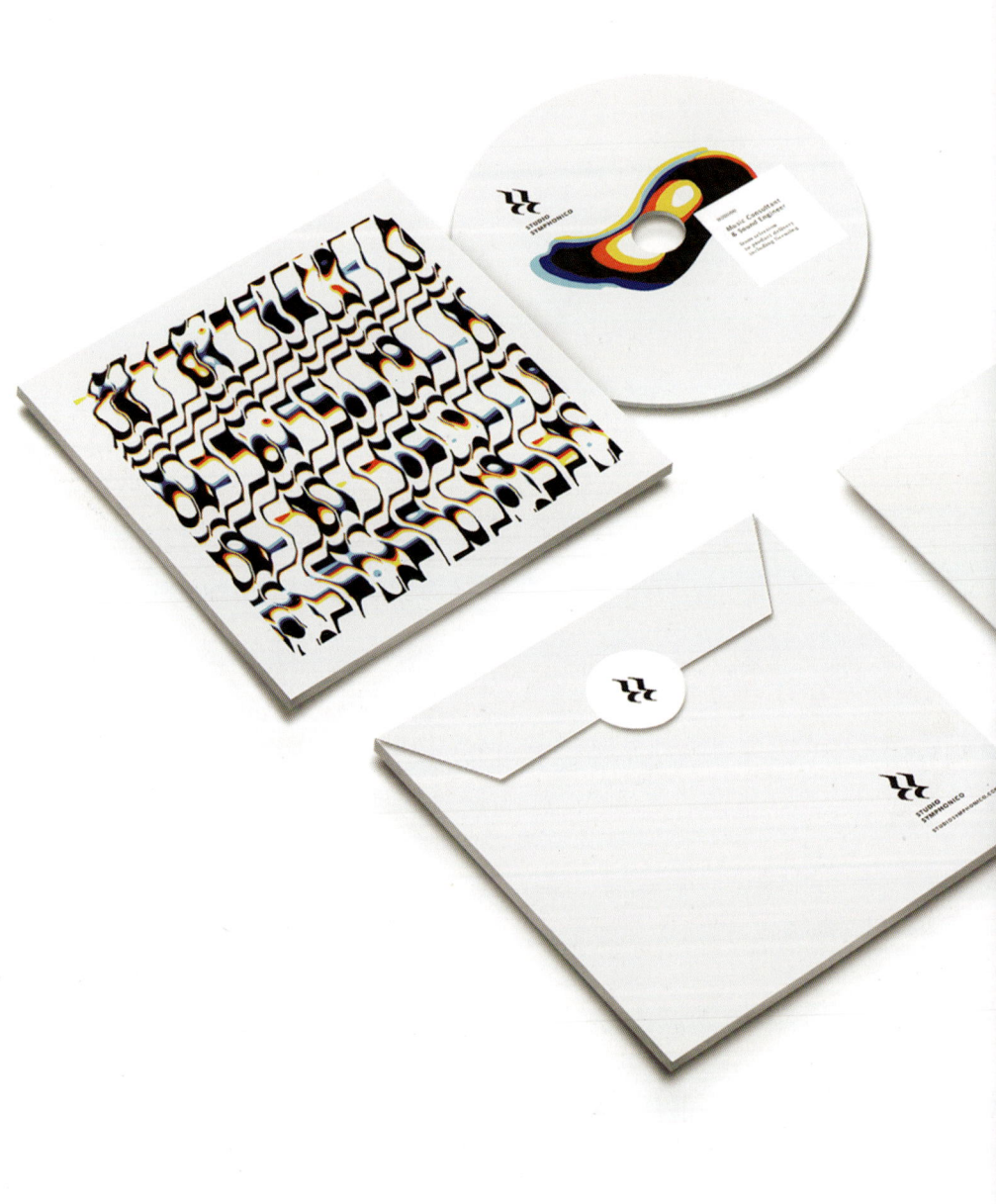

Sile, Oasi d'Acque e di Sapori is the Municipality of Treviso, Italy, where visitors can enjoy food and wine, sports, cultural events, and beautiful Venetian villas. Here, everything is nature.

Design **Kristina Nikaj**
Client **Municipality Treviso**

Sile

TASK
The aim of the logo was to recall the title of the "Sile, oasis of water and flavors," make explicit reference to the characteristics of "natural, landscape, and environmental," and be unusual, distinctive, and recognizable, representing nature and the territory.

INSPIRATIONS & CONCEPTS
The elements that most characterize the Sile include its water that comes from the earth as if by magic and its trees which can be seen everywhere. The circular shape became the essence of the project to incorporate many typical elements featuring the Sile.

FINAL SOLUTION
The final result was a logo imitating water and a tree's growth ring with a customized Bodonian typeface. The black color and the paper were chosen to add up a rough and earthy feeling.

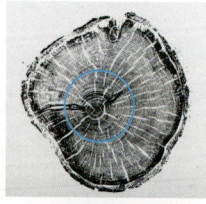

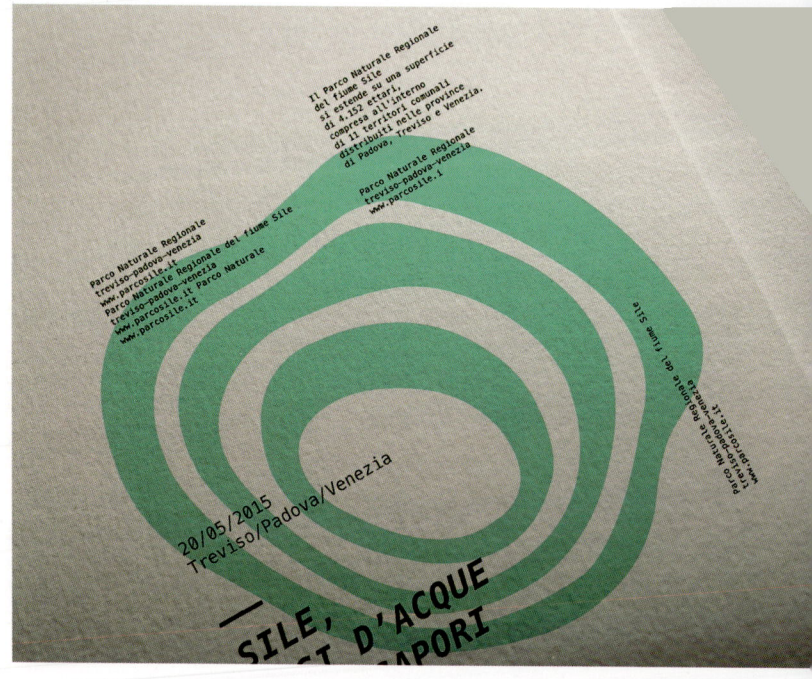

L'Éclair is a French patisserie offering delicious pastries that opened in Lisbon in May 2014.

Design **Studio WABA**
Client **L'Éclair**

L'Éclair

TASK
The team was asked to join the project by the architecture team to help with the wall decoration, but the team ended up developing all the brand communication for the patisserie which only had the logo.

INSPIRATIONS & CONCEPTS
The new concept focused mainly on eclairs.

FINAL SOLUTION
The new logo combines the circle from the original logo and waves from the pastry cream to show the special quality of the brand. The palette comes from berries, rose litchi, chocolate caramel hazelnut, and lemon pastry cream, creating a delicious and tempting atmosphere.

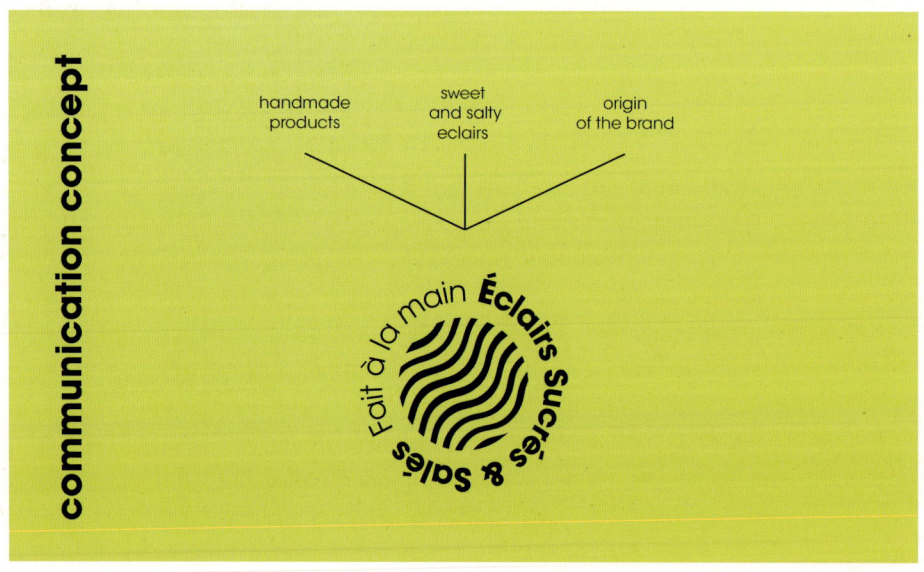

With the upcoming opening of the Museum of Contemporary Art and the National Opera, the team realised that a museum that would showcase Greek and international Art of the 20th century was important in establishing Athens as a major cultural destination. The future of the museum would be comparable in scope and vision to the ones in other major cities, displaying a comprehensive collection of international art, introducing to the audience Greek modern artists' significant contribution to the artistic achievements of the previous centuries.

Athens Museum of Modern Art

TASK

Design a contemporary, yet timeless identity for the Museum of Modern Art in Athens, that will distinguish the museum from the rest in Greece and at the same time link together a vast collection of different works from different art movements, styles, artists, and mediums.

INSPIRATIONS & CONCEPTS

The logo of the museum draws inspiration from the works of M. C. Escher and his optical illusions. The logo consists of a three dimensional cluster of the letters "M" and "T" that are the initials of the words museum, modern, and art in Greek (μουσείο, μοντέρνα, τέχνη).

FINAL SOLUTION

The primary colors of PANTONE® Orange 021C and PANTONE® 7457U were chosen to give a contemporary feel to the museum's identity and at the same time connect it to the warm colors of the Greek landscape. The font family is PF Din Text Pro, designed by Parachute Fonts (www.parachutefonts.com) in 2002, based on Din 1451 that was designed in the 1930s. The font consists of 14 different weights and a large number of glyphs, small caps, numerals, fractions, symbols, and ordinals, both in Greek and Latin.

Design **Yorgos Panagopoulos**
Photography **Dimosthenis Bitras**
Client **Athens Museum of Modern Art**
(Self-Initiated)

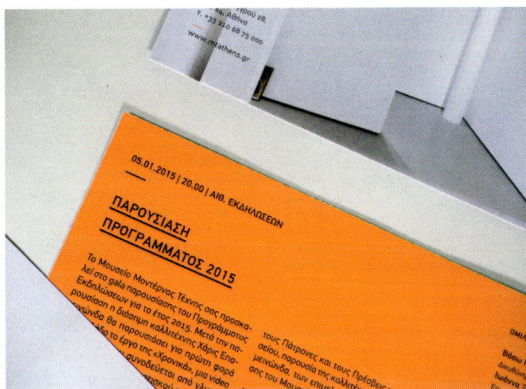

Materia means material or ingredient in Italian. Materia is a company that deals with fabric for tailored suits, run by Ditale International. The brand name conveys their goal: to grow and expand in the competitive market through the usage of the most basic and authentic materials and ingredients.

Design agency **Studio fnt**
Design **Jaemin Lee**
Client **Ditale International**

Brand Identity for Materia

TASK
Materia's request was to show the variety of fabrics they import and men's accessories they retail. They needed a design that covers both characteristics of B2B and B2C. The team tried to avoid the usual heavy and classy look of regular men's clothing or accessories stores.

INSPIRATIONS & CONCEPTS
The design started from the meaning behind the naming of the brand, Materia. The team decided to use two contrasting ideas as design elements: colorful, light, and playful inner surface V.S. outer shell with ancillary elements and a authentic look.

FINAL SOLUTION
The team split the letters in the word Materia into smaller elements of lines and surfaces. A logo was developed from this, and patterns also stemmed from the surface parts in the logo, seen when the lines are taken away. This signifies the fabric ingredient (colorful and playful inner surface) and the skills input for the making of suits (elaborate and simple outer shell – lines). Through the combination of these contrasting elements, the team managed to give the identity a mixture of authentic and cute look.

229

Nicolas Di Vittorio is a web and application developer, and also a spare time designer.

Design **Nicolas Di Vittorio**
Client **Nicolas Di Vittorio**

Nicolas D.V. – Personal Branding

TASK
Since design is an important part of his life, the designer wanted a logo that represents himself.

INSPIRATIONS & CONCEPTS
The structure should be very simple, as the designer loves simplicity.

FINAL SOLUTION
The logo started with the designer's name's initials: "N," "D," and "V." Then he used a circle, which is a shape representing simplicity, to link all the initials together.

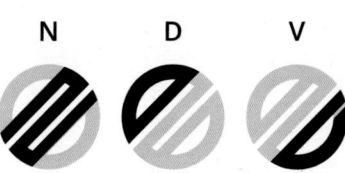

N D V + ◯ + 🧪 = ⊘

initials   simplicity   time attempts fun   result.

Jon Ander Pazos is an architect and graphic designer from Barakaldo (Biscay), who after finishing his studies of architecture in San Sebastián moves to Valencia, where he is currently based, to continue his studies with a master in multimedia design. The identity is configured so that some of the fundamental features of the brand are remarked, such as the synthesis of information without losing the meaning.

Design **Jon Ander Pazos**
Client **Jon Ander Pazos**

Personal Branding

TASK
The designer thinks it's one of the projects that he found more difficult. To him, sometimes it's much easier to do a project for another person or company than for himself. At first, he started playing with his initials, but he found everything was too simple and a little impersonal. He also tried playing with some figures of objects that make him feel represented, but they didn't convince him. Finally, the designer decided to take up a self-portrait project that he made some time ago and after passing through a process of synthesis, abstraction, and geometrization he came up with the final logo.

INSPIRATIONS & CONCEPTS
The designer has always felt inspired by the Swiss design and the Bauhaus school and their ease way to express so much with so little. When the designer was studying architecture he loved the philosophy of "less is more" from Mies Van der Rohe and the minimalism from his contemporaries. By the way, he also found inspiration in great designers and illustrators such as Saul Bass, Paul Rand, and Milton Graser, and in many people more novel who are doing great things and known on the internet.

FINAL SOLUTION
The logo was created from the abstraction and synthesis of a self image with the intention to create a more trusting relationship with potential clients. Furthermore, due to the fact that it was created from a personal image, a unique and exclusive symbol was achieved.

235

Valors is a company focused on solar power business in Japan, established in 2011.

Design agency **Enhanced Inc.**
Design **Hiromi Maeo**
Client **Valors**

Valors Rebranding

TASK
The tasks included VI construction that aimed to enhance customers' sense of security and confidence in the brand, building brand collaterals with simple and clean looks, building a corporate image reflecting the company's products and services of high quality.

INSPIRATIONS & CONCEPTS
"Valors" means "value" in Latin. In modern economics, value is defined as the nature of a product to meet the physical and mental desires of people. As people have different desires, values are divers. The design has to reflect that, as well as the company's business.

FINAL SOLUTION
The team combined three elements as metaphors of Valors: "jewelry" which symbolizes irreplaceable and valuable thing, "rainbow" which symbolizes diversity and promises, and "sun" which is the source of solar energy.

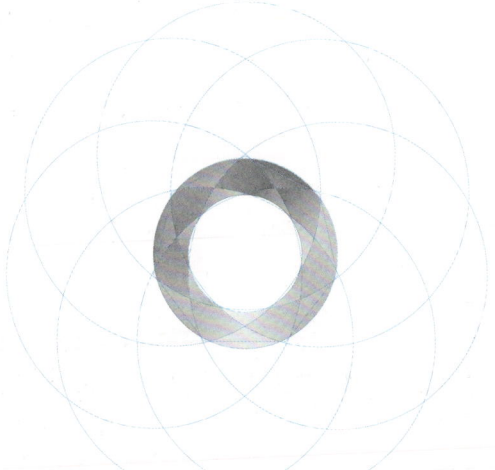

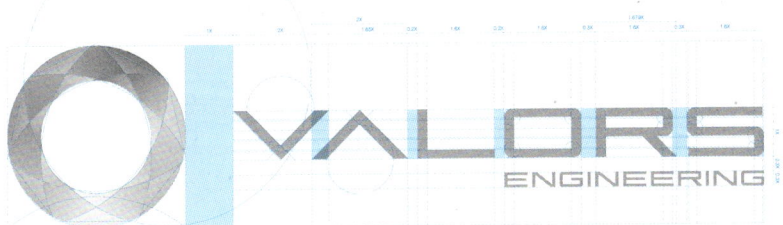

Golden Ratio=1:1.618

MTRL, short for Material and created by Loftwork Inc., is a cafe, an event space, and a personal fabrication workshop. It also serves as a gallery showcasing Kyoto-made materials, offers Airbnb lodging, and functions as Loftwork's Kyoto office.

Design agency **Enhanced Inc.**
Design **Hiromi Maeo**
Client **Loftwork Inc.**

MTRL KYOTO New Identity

TASK
New VI design and art direction for MTRL.

INSPIRATIONS & CONCEPTS
MTRL logo is composed of a combination of four "material symbols." The simplified designs aim to awaken and stimulate people's imagination. The "material symbol" is made up of a 10 × 10 grid. This grid came about partly to achieve pixel perfection, but mostly to symbolize the fundamental bits to atoms essence of the Maker Movement. Each and every one of the squares that make up the "material Symbols" are a bit (the smallest unit of digital information), and when these bits are combined together they become "material." The individual bits themselves are also "material."

FINAL SOLUTION
The combination of material symbols created the logo with a simple shape but also visually unique.

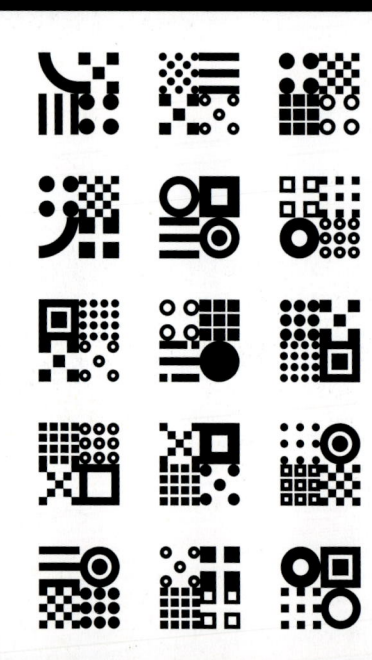

 |

 |

ABCDEFGHIJ
KLMNOPQRS
TUVWXYZ.,/:
0123456789

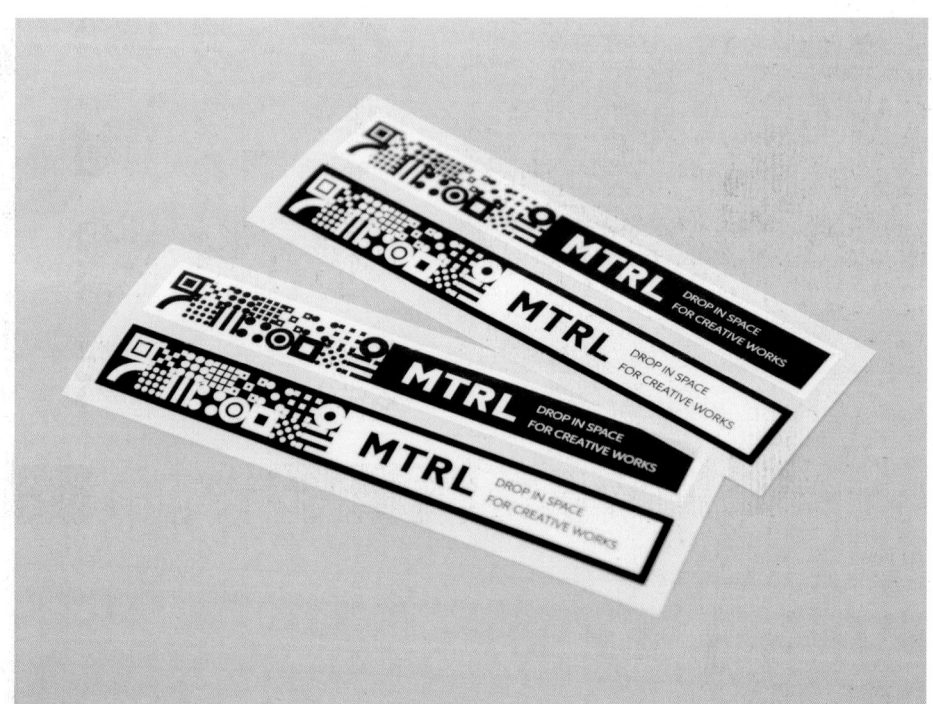

Interview   Hiromi Maeo - Enhanced Inc.

Tell me a little about your studio. How did it start? What do you do?
I started as Enhanced in 2012. Before that, I worked for several design studios.
   Currently, Enhanced Inc. focuses on design production related to branding, including logo development, etc.
   Our designs are mainly graphics, web, and UI/UX, and may also include some space design.

Is branding a big part of your activity?
Yes. Corporate branding is our main activity.

What type of information do you usually gather from the client before starting a logo and branding project?
Usually, interviews focus on information such as the history and vision of the brand, the thoughts of the founder, and the world that the brand aims to create.
   Based on this information, core keywords are extracted.
   We then develop a concept, after which we compile design ideas.

Where do you find inspiration for your work in branding and logo design?
Keywords extracted from interviews are the main source of inspiration.
   I sometimes get hints from casual events in my daily life, my son playing, conversations with friends, etc.

Could you give me a couple of examples of the branding projects you feel most proud of?
MTRL KYOTO Coworking space

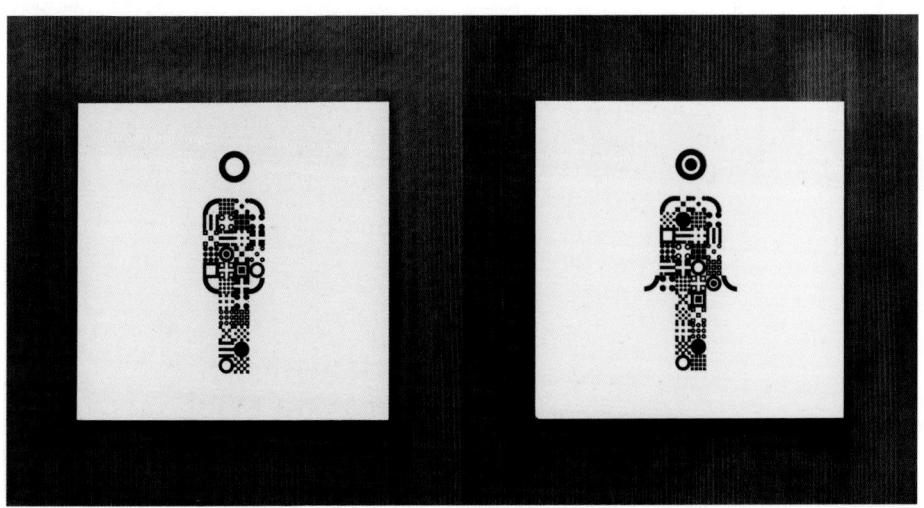

The project won several awards.
MTRL is growing significantly as a business.
https://www.behance.net/gallery/28289535/MTRL-KYOTO-New-Identity

GAZE - 浙商总会
Logo development project for an organization chaired by Jack Ma, founder of Alibaba Group.
   About 10 design studios from around the world were nominated and a competition was held. This logo was ultimately selected.
https://www.behance.net/gallery/32149453/GAZE-

JP GAMES
Logo design project for the new company of Hajime Tabata, one of the most famous game producers in the world.
https://www.jpgamesinc.com/

In addition, there is a project related to a new business for a major Japanese airline company. I feel very proud of this project with the airline company, as it has been a long-cherished dream of mine. Unfortunately, however, this project cannot be made public due to client compliance.

What are the most challenging and most rewarding parts of designing a brand?
Creating the concept is the most challenging and most rewarding part. Because the concept is the basis for all designs.

Rebels Studios is an independent production studio based in Stockholm focusing on film, design, and digital. They do work and collaborations with ad agencies, big brands and businesses as well as smaller start ups, record labels, and artists. Rebels Studios exists because they value the freedom to experiment, play, and explore. Their philosophy is to create qualified work while having a good time doing it. Rebels Studios' people always keep this in mind when it comes to how they work and the people they work with.

Rebels Studios Branding

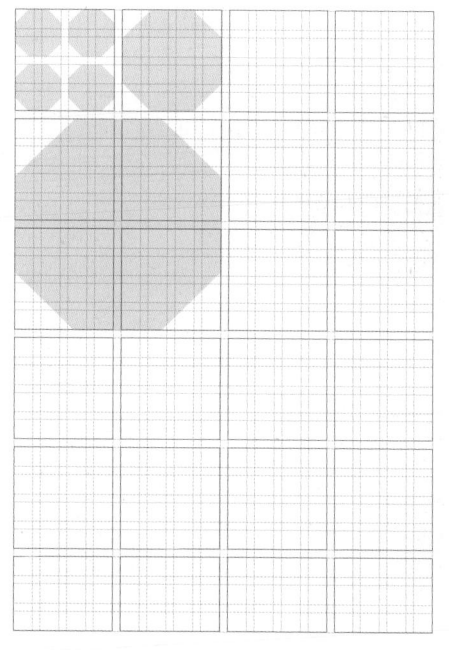

TASK
Create a new branding that represents the studio's three main areas: film, design, and digital.

INSPIRATIONS & CONCEPTS
The team drew inspirations from structures, Lego, building blocks, camera equipments, and technology.

FINAL SOLUTION
The studio was in the process of taking a new direction enhancing the three main areas of expertise film, design, and digital to provide a clearer vision and approach. The final result was a new symbol that consists of three building blocks, forming the letters r & s. The shape of the blocks was inspired by the shapes and angles of camera rigs — since they do a lot of filming and that's where it all started. Later on the team also added design and digital in the mix.

Design agency **Rebels Studios**
Design **Filip Kleremark**
Client **Rebels Studios**

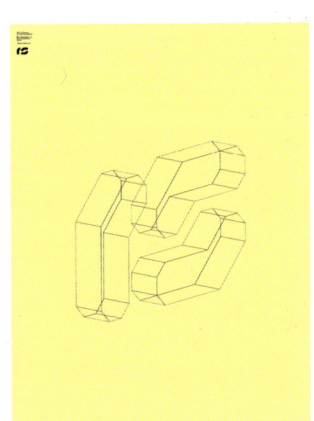

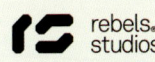

251

Entre-Tintas is a printer based in Bilbao, Spain.

Design agency **Happyending Studio**
Design **Ángela Alonso & Elena Perea**
Client **Parima Digital S.L.**

Entre-Tintas

TASK
In 2013, the team was asked to rename the company and develop a corporate identity for it.

INSPIRATIONS & CONCEPTS
The team has never worked on a name before, so that was not an easy task for them. After a very long search for words or expressions that could clearly connect the company to the field of printing, the team came across the name "entre-tintas (between-inks)."

FINAL SOLUTION
After the renaming, the team soon became aware of the fact that the name they had built contained an "E" and a "T." They started working with an ampersand straight away, and tried to develop a logo that would be a literal translation of the name. To create an effect of made of several layers of black ink, stripes were used to draw the shape of their ampersand. The space between those "ink layers" would always be left blank. They also decided to surround the sign with a circle, as a reference for a color halftone. As basic principles to accompany the logo and develop the rest of the identity, the team had two main concepts: a simple color palette as a representation of the act of mixing basic colors to get new ones, and a dot-based pattern as a connection to the act of printing itself.

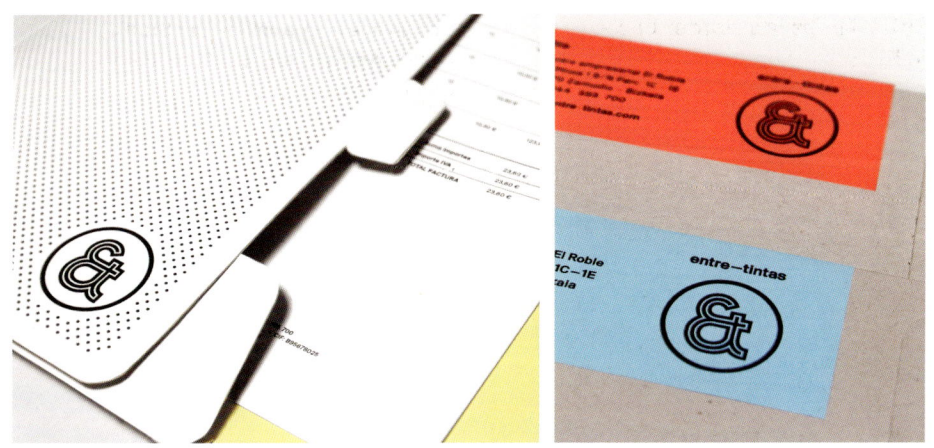

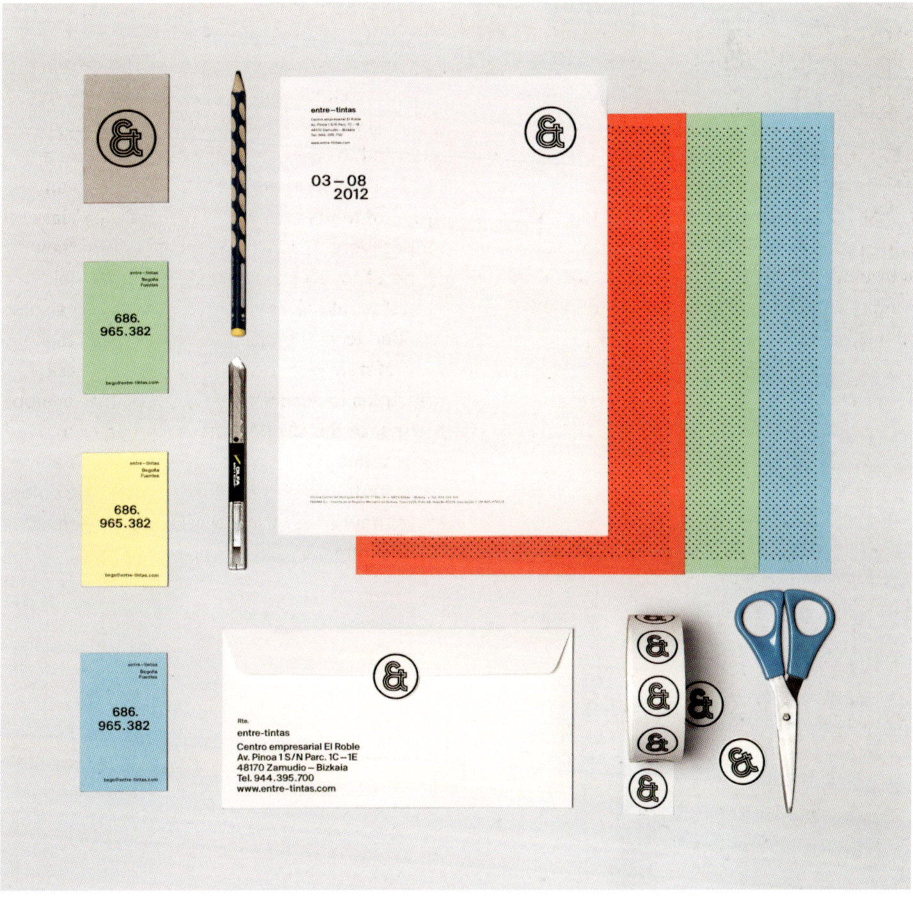

"Chasha Tepla" is a small group of people driven by the same ideas and keen on good Chinese tea. They sell and deliver elite sorts of tea in Saint-Petersburg.

Design **Masaomi Fujita**
Client **Plows Farm & Other Things**

Chasha Tepla Branding

TASK
The task included the creation of the name and a dynamic logo of the company, as well as the basis of corporate identity.

INSPIRATIONS & CONCEPTS
Chinese characters and eastern symbols expressing unique eastern spirit.

FINAL SOLUTION
The interlinear translation of the name is "the bowl of warmth" but the design team suggested "Cozy Cup" as the English title. The name reflects the heartfulness and the spirituality, typical implications for this eastern drink. The design that consists of simple elements such as water, steam, tea leaf, cup, and fire shaped by the lines of the same thickness supports this feeling. The final solution included the simple images formed by thin lines, hieroglyphs, mono chromaticism, characteristic typography showing the contrast of two different fonts (the bold grotesque of the name of the brand and the antique of the rest of the text), exaggerated freedom of compositional collocations, and simple natural materials of the medium. The business cards were printed using a silk-screen on a cardboard, which consists of 100% recycled paper.

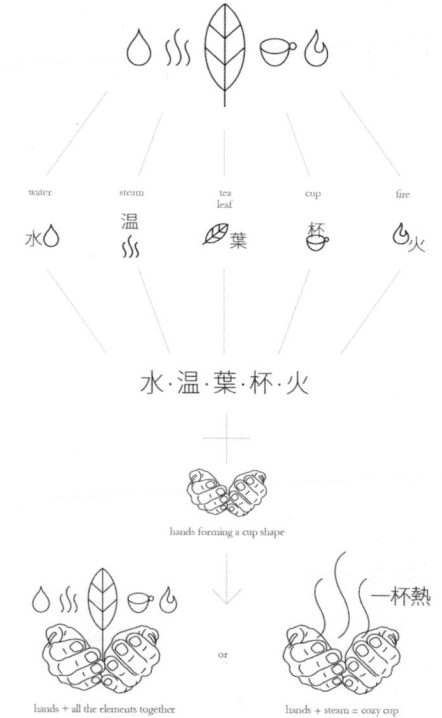

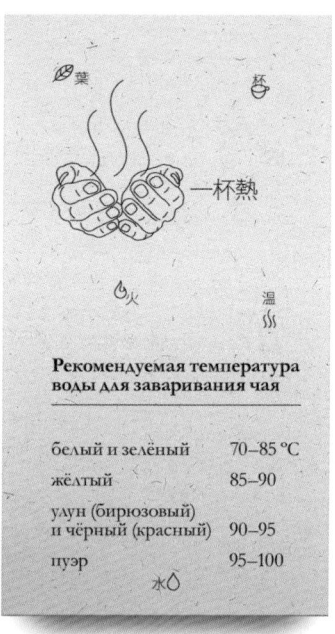

белый и зелёный	70–85 °C
жёлтый	85–90
улун (бирюзовый) и чёрный (красный)	90–95
пуэр	95–100

"Plows" was named for the individual business by Mr. Shingo Kikuchi who has been living on manual custom-made leather shoes and bags. He works for agriculture at the same time.

Design **Masaomi Fujita**
Client **Plows Farm & Other Things**

Plows

TASK
The team was offered to create a visual identity and business name. They needed to represent his two business styles – "a farmer" and "a leather craftsman" in the name at the same time.

INSPIRATIONS & CONCEPTS
The team found the common key word "plows," meaning being able to cultivate a new business soil and also doing great as a farmer.

FINAL SOLUTION
Finally, the team designed his business name logo and business card. The business card has an embossing of hoe as symbolizing "plows."

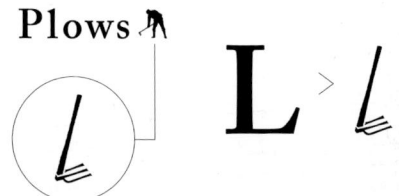

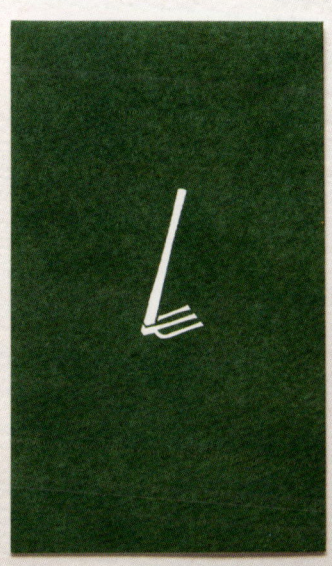

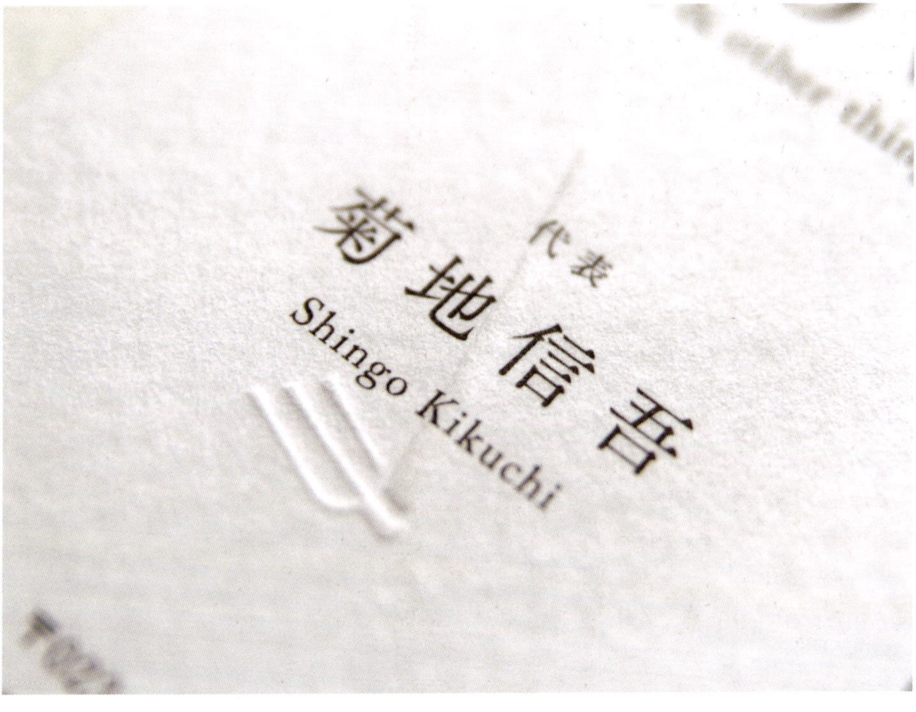

Aryana Tatum is a metal smith based in Oakland, California. Her work includes jewelry, metal sculptures, and art objects which respond to both beauty and function.

Design **Natalia Bivol**
Client **Aryana Tatum**

Aryana Tatum Jewelry and Metal Arts Identity

TASK
The goal of the project was to create a new identity that will better represent the jeweler's work and artistic personality.

INSPIRATIONS & CONCEPTS
Aryana maintained an architectural approach to her designs keeping the focus on the structure, dynamic, geometry, and modularity. The designer drew inspiration from it.

FINAL SOLUTION
The designer combined 4 "A"s and 2 "T"s, which are the initials of "Aryana" and "Tatum," to make a logo imitating the structure of a jewelry. Black was chosen as it is a color representing eternity. The designer also explored different logo lockup options that would apply to the website, packaging, collaterals, and social media.

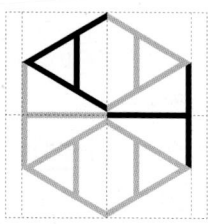

258

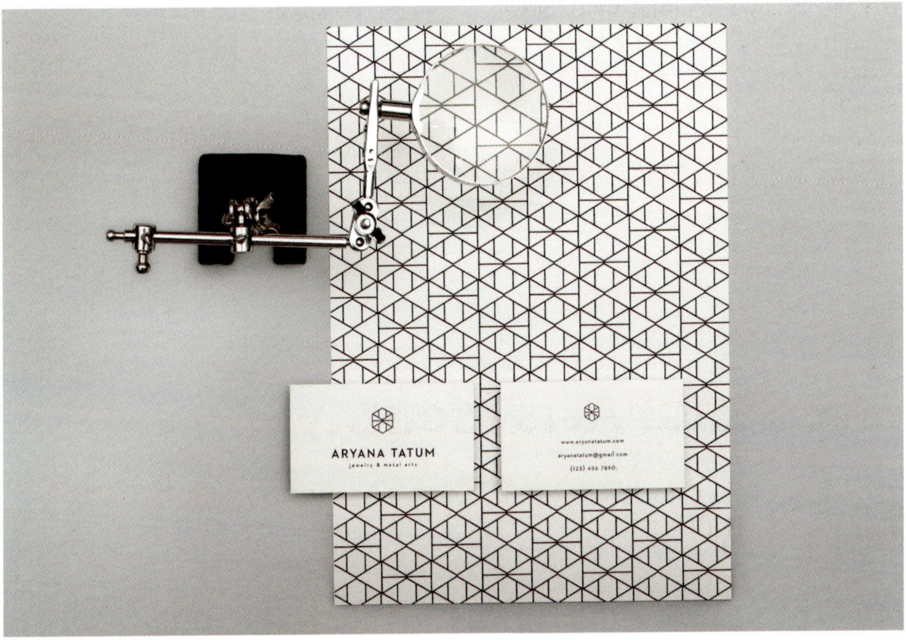
ARYANA TATUM
jewelry & metal arts
www.aryanatatum.com
aryanatatum@gmail.com
(123) 456 7890

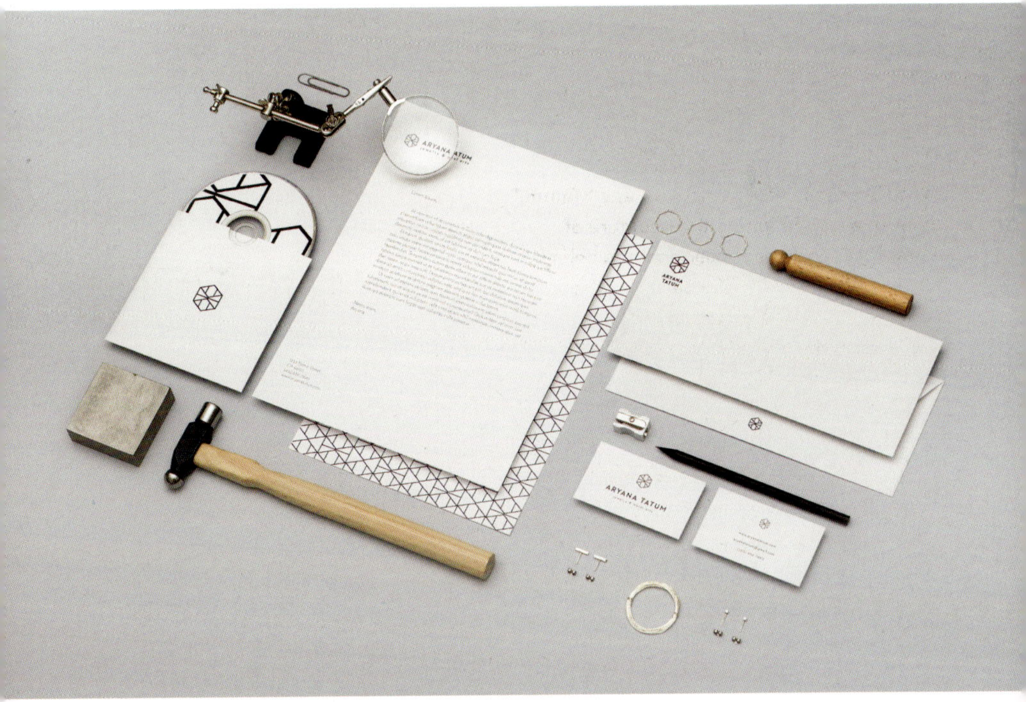
ARYANA TATUM

FAUPÈ is an apparel brand established in 2015 by Vanessa Jashanica.

Design **Dawid Cmok**
Client **FAUPÈ**

FAUPÈ

TASK
Create a brand identity for FAUPÈ to showcase its unique character.

INSPIRATIONS & CONCEPTS
In popular culture, deer symbolizes endurance, persistence, vitality, and ability to focus on goals. The designer decided to use this symbol to represent the inner spirit of the brand.

FINAL SOLUTION
FAUPÈ's symbol consists of a visual representation of a deer head with antlers and the name of the company. The logo is simple, clean, and geometric. Its symmetrical form represents balance. It has a bold and audacious feel that illustrates the keynote of the brand. The designer also created elements of branding identity including logotype variants, letterheads, envelopes, business cards, graphic patterns, accessories, and a responsive website.

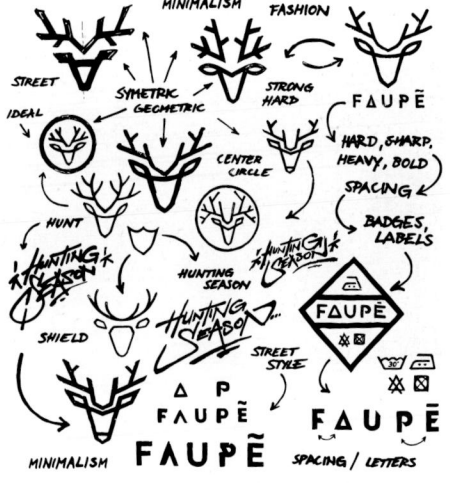

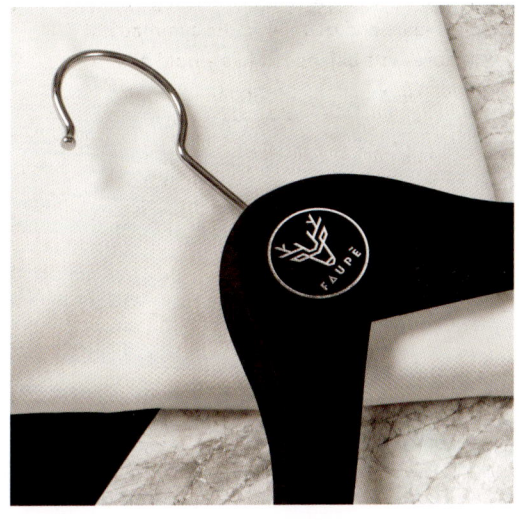

Wooden Kingdom

TASK
The author was asked to create a distinctive image for the lumberjack's brand.

INSPIRATIONS & CONCEPTS
The design was based on a functional and minimalist approach.

FINAL SOLUTION
The designer chose a bear as the main visual as bear represents some qualities that a lumberjack has, like being strong, powerful, and persistent. Within his work the author created elements of branding identity including logotype variants, letterheads, envelopes, visiting cards, accessories, and an identity book.

Nolio is a restaurant located in Krakow, Poland, inspired by the Italian way of life, mentality, imagination, and hospitality. Nolio promotes a culture of eating and enjoying one's social life, and honor the life attitude of hedonism. Its menu is composed as Italian dinner, consisting of many dishes and celebrated for hours.

Dishes are created from fine Italian products, from traditional and organic family farming.

Design **Nina Gregier, Piotr Wojtaszek**
Client **Nolio Restaurant**

Nolio

TASK
The main task was to design a very simple visual identity which will bring the food to the fore.

INSPIRATIONS & CONCEPTS
Strong block letters and slender use of color.

FINAL SOLUTION
The visual Identity for Nolio was based on typography and underlines. The team used only black color and applied it on a wide range of natural and recycled papers. Silkscreen print gave it a rawer look. Additionally, the team had several Ns designed specifically for Nolio. The result was an identity that is strong and easy to apply on various media (printed, embroidered, carved, etc.).

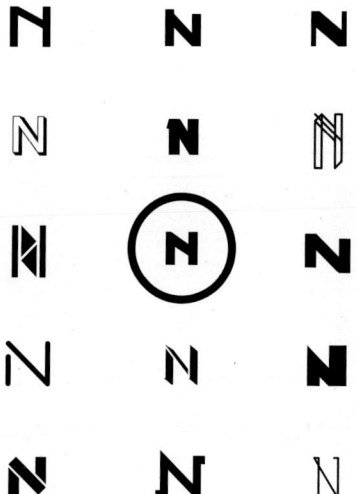

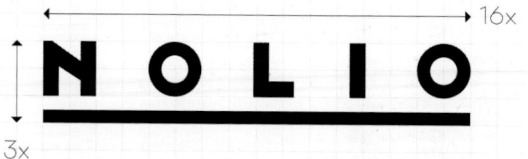

The Saloon is a British-inspired cafe, bar, and restaurant located in Tokyo that still retains the industrial feel of London's original Covent Garden marketplace. The menu spans from modern British cooking with an emphasis on traditional homemade style to specialty beers and drinks from UK.

Design **Studio Newwork**
Client **The Saloon**

The Saloon

TASK
Studio Newwork was assigned to create the comprehensive brand identity system including logo, store card, coffee cup, paper napkin, receipt, and signage.

INSPIRATIONS & CONCEPTS
The inspirations came from traditional British pubs and novel British cuisine.

FINAL SOLUTION
The solution was a classic typographic approach with a modern twist. The apex of "A" in "SALOON" meets horizontally to give a sense of a secret traditional British pub, while the contemporary lime green color represents a fresh, non-traditional side of British cuisine.

THE SALOON
—
UNIQUE WINES · BEERS & MEALS

Located in Paris downtown, in a pedestrian street behind Beaubourg, the Underclub aims to be the new techno-lovers' HQ. Every collective will appropriate the place with their music, in an intimate space which can welcome up to 300 people.

Design **Studio Gris**
Photography **Laura Perez**
Client **SARL Campoix**

Underclub Paris

TASK
The team had to create the whole identity and the graphics standards for the club and the events including logotype, colors, flyers, posters, illustrations, website, etc.

INSPIRATIONS & CONCEPTS
The club which hosted the Detroit-techno pioneers such as the Magic Stick and the Music Institute shares the same architectural tendencies with other specialized clubs: big disused buildings, long rectangular windows, and Bauhaus uprightness. It is this rigor, associated to industrial techno sounds, that the team tried to graphically re-transcribe.

FINAL SOLUTION
The team created a type logo with a specific arrangement working on the relation between full and empty spaces. Some graphic patterns can complete the logotype and create different variations. The graphics standards are associated with the illustrations they made and the Bosun type using only lowercases.

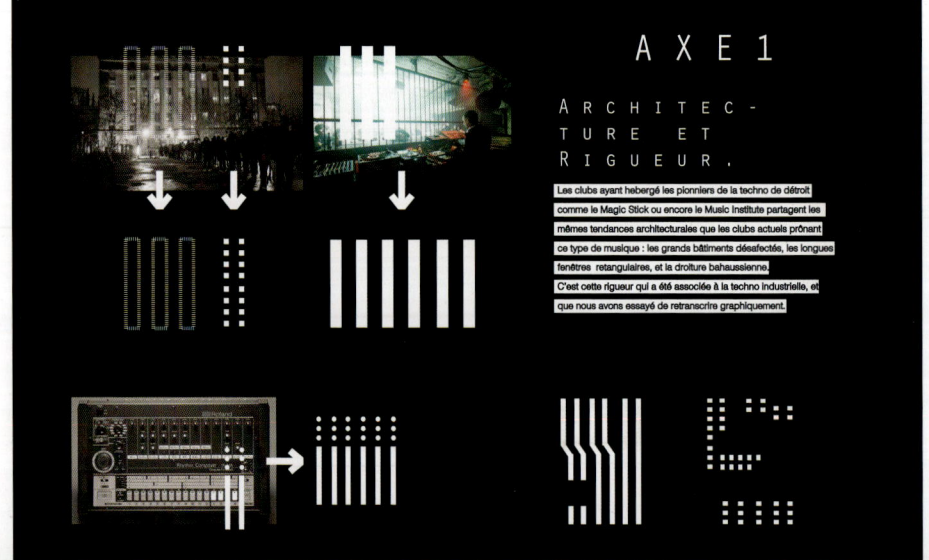

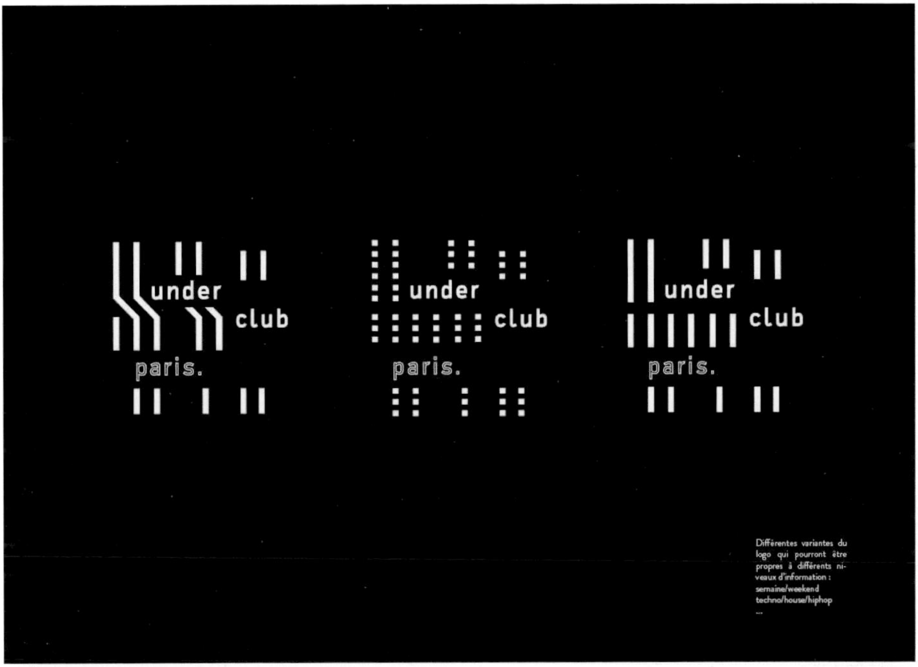

Différentes variantes du logo qui pourront être propres à différents niveaux d'information :
semaine/weekend
techno/house/hiphop
...

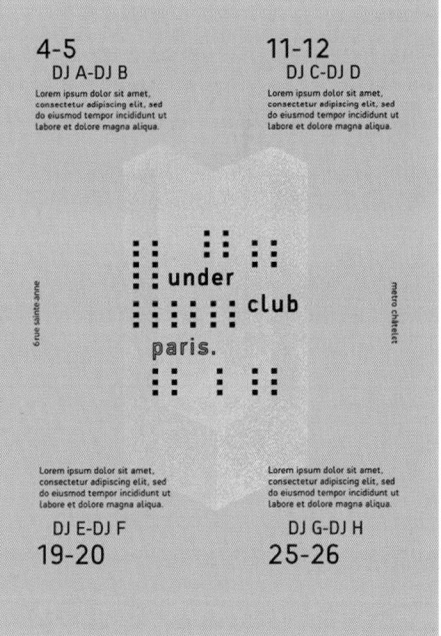

Ano Viannos is a small village in south Crete, historically famous for German's slaughter to it in 1943. During the mass executions, among hundreds of people, Stathis Mastoras was killed. As a known composer of Greek operetta, Stathis starred in the musical theater during late '20s and '30s. He was also a teacher, a scientist, and a poet. This small chorus is dedicated to his memory.

Design **Kalambokis Demetris**
Client **Ano Viannos Cultural Center & Chorus**

Viannos Chorus Branding

TASK
The chorus was set up in November 2013 with 30 members. It serves as a cultural oasis for Ano Viannos. To gain financial support, the secretariat decided to create a basic corporate ID to strengthen and raise the local's willingness to participate. Viannos Cultural Center decided to use the composer's name for the chorus and the final logo.

INSPIRATIONS & CONCEPTS
The Cultural Center of Ano Viannos needed a logotype that should involve from either a specific history milestone of the village (refer to: WWII), or the work of Stathis Mastoras, the famous opera composer, or even a traditional reference on Cretan culture. After several designs, the music concept prevailed among the other two ideas.

FINAL SOLUTION
The final design was based on two main elements: the composer's hand holding his baton and the chorus music book. The custom-made typeface used for the acronym CVSM (original: ΧΒΣΜ) was combined with the idea of a stringed instrument to give the logo greater freedom. The concept of the chorus book was depicted on a straight lined pattern. The three colored books with that "pattern" indicate the three chorus sections: child, youth, and adult department.

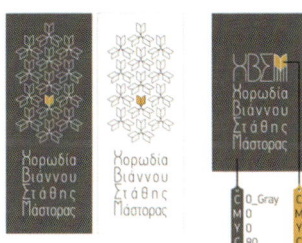
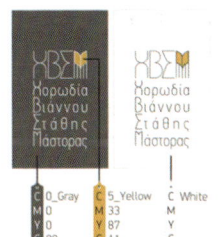

Stickers, Stamps, Other Applications

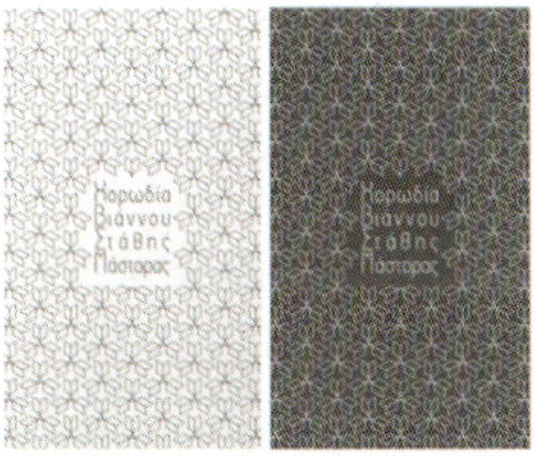

Identity Cards, Envelopes, etc

Choir Holding a Book For "Compliments" & Packaging

Myth Clothing is a new fashion brand. Their clothes are a bit baroque, yet casual. They also make film costumes.

Design **Nina Gregier**
Client **Myth Clothing**

Myth Clothing

TASK
The task was to design a logotype as simple as possible with a funny "magical" twist.

INSPIRATIONS & CONCEPTS
The designer drew inspirations from objects with a magical touch like lion and diamond.

FINAL SOLUTION
The logo was based on two geometrical symbols: lion as a mythical animal and diamond as a magic stone. Typography is very simple and color contains palette of grey. There are a lot of additional symbols, made of font glyphs. The result was an interesting logo, simple in form but rich in meaning. Also it is easy to apply on various media.

MYTH

Heaven and hell are within us, and all the gods are within us.

This is the great realization of the Upanishads of India in the ninth Century B.C. All the gods, all the heavens, all the world, are within us.

They are magnified dreams, and dreams are manifestations in image form of the energies of the body in conflict with each other.

That is what myth is.

— JOSEPH CAMPBELL, THE POWER OF MYTH

MYTHOLOGY IS NOT A LIE.
MYTHOLOGY IS POETRY,
IT IS METAPHORICAL.

IT HAS BEEN WELL SAID THAT MYTHOLOGY IS THE PENULTIMATE TRUTH — PENULTIMATE BECAUSE THE ULTIMATE CANNOT BE PUT INTO WORDS.

IT IS BEYOND WORDS.

— JOSEPH CAMPBELL, THE POWER OF MYTH

READ MYTHS.
THEY TEACH YOU.
THAT YOU CAN TURN INWARD,
AND YOU BEGIN TO GET THE
MESSAGE OF THE SYMBOLS.
MYTH HELPS YOU
TO PUT YOUR MIND IN TOUCH
WITH THIS EXPERIENCE
OF BEING ALIVE.

— JOSEPH CAMPBELL, THE POWER OF MYTH

Love   is the burning point of
           life, and since
           all life is sorrowful,
           so is love.
The stronger the love,
           the more the pain.
           Love itself is pain,
           you might say
           — the pain of
           being truly alive.

— JOSEPH CAMPBELL, THE POWER OF MYTH

I BELIEVE IN EVERYTHING
UNTIL IT'S DISPROVED.
SO I BELIEVE IN FAIRIES,
THE MYTHS, DRAGONS.

IT ALL EXISTS,
EVEN IF IT'S IN
YOUR MIND.
WHO'S TO SAY
THAT DREAMS
AND NIGHTMARES
AREN'T AS REAL
AS THE HERE AND NOW?

— JOHN LENNON

MYTH BASICALLY SERVES FOUR FUNCTIONS.

THE FIRST IS THE MYSTICAL FUNCTION.

REALIZING

WHAT A WONDER THE UNIVERSE IS,
AND WHAT A WONDER YOU ARE,
AND EXPERIENCING
ARE BEFORE THIS MYSTERY.

— JOSEPH CAMPBELL, THE POWER OF MYTH

MISARA is a clothing brand based in Canary Islands.

Design **Pablo Chico**
Client **MISARA**

MISARA

TASK
Create a visual system for the brand.

INSPIRATIONS & CONCEPTS
The designer drew inspirations from the products the brand is selling, the initial letter of the brand's name, and its global branding strategy.

FINAL SOLUTION
The designer combined the above elements to create a minimal and humorous logo to present the character of the brand.

 + M + O = Ⓜ̈

DRESSED UP   LETTER "M"   GLOBAL

 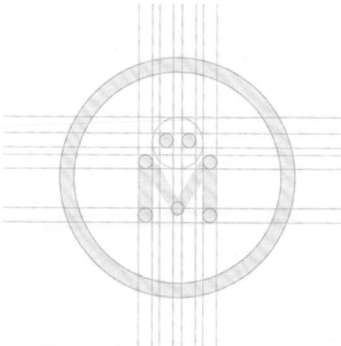

Olivia is an urban bistro based in Mexico.

Design **Fer Cuenca**
Client **Olivia Bistró Urbano**

Olivia Bistró Urbano

TASK
Create a sophisticated and casual identity for the brand.

INSPIRATIONS & FINAL SOLUTIONS
An urban style is conveyed through the use of metals and textures, including copper, which is an essential element used in the restaurant's decoration. The logo's design is simple and elegant, and uses a modest stenciled "urban" detail. The designer particularly enjoyed creating artistic posters for the restaurant, which will also be used as flyers. All of the identity presents the same mixture of sophisticated and urban style.

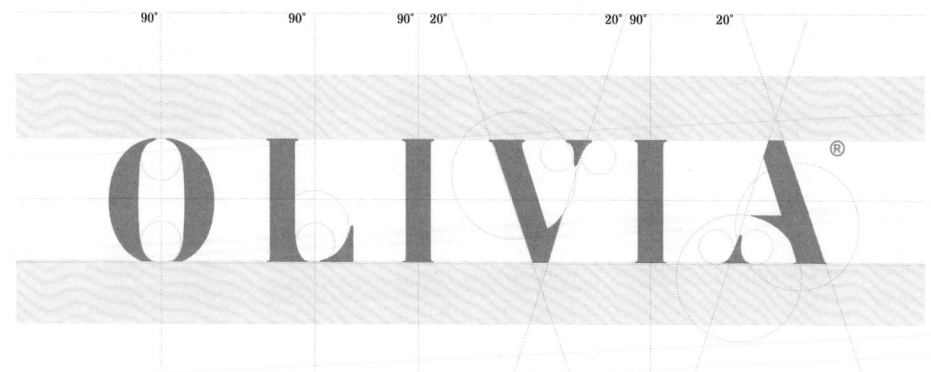

OLIVIA®

BISTRÓ URBANO

Acto is a construction company based in Lajeado, Rio Grande do Sul, Brazil. They bring together the best professionals, the most skilled partners, and modern construction practices to deliver unique projects for their clients.

Design agency **Frente**
Design **Carlos Paaschen, Germano Redecker, Rodrigo Brod, Vagner Zarpellon**
Photography **Giovane Sebastiany**
Client **Acto**

Acto

TASK
Create a name, logo, and visual identity that translate in a simple and sophisticated way the experience of buying a new home. The logo should work in one color and on a variety of surfaces by different materials.

INSPIRATIONS & CONCEPTS
Inspired by architecture and the elements of houses, like roofs, keys and in the "keyhole effect," the team used simple forms to create all the letters that together formed this unique logo.

FINAL SOLUTION
The logo and visual identity developed were based on simple forms that translate the meaningful feeling of arriving in a new home, implicit in the "keyhole effect" presented in the letters C and O, and in the geometrical architecture of roofs and keys presented in the letters A and T, respectively. All the material choices and printing processes were conducted to enhance the tactile experience. The stationery designed for Acto uses textured paper, embossing, and screen printing to ensure the desired look and feel.

284

Donnybrook Studio is a newly built creative space served as an activity centre for young people in Dublin to spend their time.

Design **Conor Smyth**
Client **Donnybrook Studio**

Donnybrook Studio Branding

TASK
The brief was to create a modern brand that might appeal to the hipster class.

INSPIRATIONS & CONCEPTS
The designer drew inspirations from the idea of "the hipster" and what they stand for. They like to break trends, go against the grain, and be different and cool.

FINAL SOLUTION
The designer created a movement effect on his logo along with a bold confident font and a modern color palette to represent the hipsters' spirit.

Prospiti is a furniture factory focused on producing furniture of high quality and unique design.

Design agency **H3L Studio**
Design **Juan Cruz Castro**
Creative direction **Horacio Lardiés**
Client **Prospiti Furniture Factory**

Prospiti Branding

TASK
Corporate branding and stationery design for Prospiti Furniture Factory.

INSPIRATIONS & CONCEPTS
This graphic system was based on Bauhaus' morphology and design concept, as well as its leading artists. Inspired by Ludwig Mies van der Rohe, the team intervened in his work and turned the chair upside down.

FINAL SOLUTION
After countless attempts in trying to find a connection between an object and a symbol, truth was revealed. The outcome was a letter "P," stripped and perfect. The warmth of leather married the coldness of steel, while the right proportion was expressed in harmony. A simple line was printed on paper and cardboards, inviting the viewers to become part of a new space that holds a design manifesto.

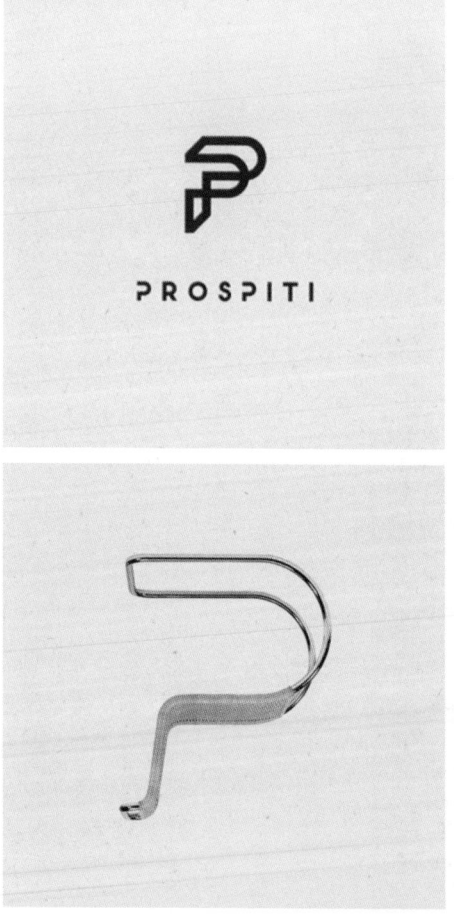

Designers' Index

303 Design Squadron
303design.com.br
A Brazilian-based design studio specialized in visual communication, whose efforts are strongly focused on branding identity building.
pp. 178-181

Alexandre Pietra
behance.net/AlexandrePietra
A young graphic designer graduated from the ERACOM (School of Arts and Communication) in Lausanne, Switzerland. He studied graphic design for 4 years in an advertising agency. To him, graphic design is not just a job, but a passion. Adept in his job, curious about graphic trends, he likes to create new visual worlds. Precision and reflection are his watchwords for works of great visual and artistic quality.
pp. 104-105

All Design Transparent
adestradesign.com
All Design Transparent (ADESTRA) is a multidisciplinary design studio located in the city centre of Saint Petersburg, specializing in branding, art direction, and user experiences. It stands out with its ability to produce complex works that cover different media. The key value for them is the quality up to a high standard, which is gained by cooperation with the best printing houses. The studio was founded by young yet talented designer Anastasia Yakovleva who's got a keen eye on design principles and is also known for precise task solutions.
pp. 156-157

Andriy Yurchenko
andyur.com
Andriy Yurchenko is a freelance designer, who primarily specializes in web-design, brand identity, and UI/UX.
pp. 182-185

Apofenia
Apofenia.co
A design studio crafting symbol-intensive brands. They use the phenomenon known as Apophenia to make connections where there were none, to organize chaos, and make the world intelligible. To them, it is useful to create ideas in their clients' mind, and to set the dots for their clients to connect.
pp. 58-59, 114-117

Bravo
bravo.rocks
Bravo is a creative studio that makes and shapes brands that matter. It develops concepts with more boldness than Arial Bold, does art direction with more artistry than Game of Thrones, and produces designs with more finesse than Anna Wintour's hair. Bravo's people love what they do.
pp. 52-57, 174-177

Chris Edwards
behance.net/chris_david_edwards
A British born designer who has always pursued a sense of physicality and meaning within his designs that reinforce the purpose, whether they are for solo or collaborative efforts. He is specialized in brand identity, editorial design, and typography. Design for

him started as a hobby, and transformed into a life style with seemingly endless roads of opportunity and experience.

pp. 190-191

Cloudtrap Design Studio

cloudtrap.gr

Cloudtrap Design Studio was founded in 2011 by Fedon Arvanitakis in Athens. It is an independent studio specializing in branding corporate identity and packaging. The purpose of the studio is to provide clever suggestions in visual communication, to make a product or a brand stand out for its style and simplicity. On the axes of minimalism and clean-cut design, they create brands that communicate the philosophy of the company, of both the client and the studio.

pp. 38-41

Conor Smyth

conorsmythdesigns.com

The designer decided to pursue a career in graphic design in 2010 and graduated in 2013 with a Bachelor of Arts in graphic design. The year he graduated he won the award for best student in the department of design and creative media. He is a huge fan of gaming and gaming culture. In his spare time, he enjoys creating fan art for some of his favorite games.

pp. 286-287

Daniel Farò, Lisa-Marie Kaspar

daniellucasfaro.com
lisamariekaspar.de

Daniel Farò and Lisa-Marie Kaspar are both photographers and fellow graphic design students from Würzburg, Germany. Daniel's style is primarily clean but colorful. He has got a strong sense for aesthetics and finds great solutions through experimenting. Lisa-Marie always likes to explore and try different styles. Her work is mainly based on clarity and structure.

pp. 68-71

Dawid Cmok

behance.net/dawidcmok

A graphic designer from Zabrze, Poland with a MFA degree in graphic design at the Academy of Fine Arts in Katowice. Graphic design and street art are the designer's passion. Every day he is looking for inspiration around him. His works have been featured in many books, magazines, and websites on graphic design around the world.

pp. 126-127, 260-267

Eliane Cadieux

elianecadieux.com

With her undone blonde locks, oversized white T-Shirt, and her loyal dog companion Walter, the designer just needs a little long weekend in the forest or with her foot in the sand to be happy. As a young designer (26 years old) living in Montreal, Quebec, Eliane is passionate about design but also about the outdoor world.

pp. 78-81, 86-87

Fabrica

fabrica.it

Fabrica is a communication research centre. It is based in Treviso, Italy, and is an integral part of the Benetton Group. Established in 1994 from a vision of Luciano Benetton, Fabrica offers young people from around the world a one-year scholarship, accommodation, and a round-trip ticket to Italy, enabling a highly diverse group of researchers. The range of disciplines is equally diverse, including design, visual communication, photography, interaction, video, music, and journalism. Fabrica is based in a campus centered on a 17th-century villa, restored and significantly augmented by renowned Japanese architect Tadao Ando.

pp. 92-95

Felix Kraus

felixkraus.net

A 24-year-old Germany-based graphic designer graduated in 2015 as Bachelor of Arts with honors in Mediadesign at the DHBW Ravensburg and based in Bavaria. He is currently working as a graphic designer for Teamsport Apparel at the sport company giant PUMA SE.

pp. 186-189

Fer Cuenca

fercuenca.com

A graphic designer based in Buenos Aires, Argentina.

pp. 282-283

Fetén STUDIO

fetenstudio.com

Fetén is a Spain-based graphic design studio specialized in creative branding solutions, co-founded by Sara Bautista and Alex de la Fuente. Their claim is "Fetén, is more than well."

pp. 72-73

Freddy Agostini

behance.net/freddyagostini

Freddy Agostini is an art director and a CGI visual designer who is effective in 3D visuals, ad campaigns, and branding with a bachelor's degree in graphic design and advertising. He is creative and resourceful in generating new ideas and solving problems, confident and decisive under stressful conditions. He was born in the USA and currently lives in Ecuador.

pp. 34-37

Frente

frente.cc

Frente is a creative studio based in Brazil. The team uses strategy, culture, and sensibility to deliver breakthrough solutions focused on design.

pp. 284-285

Gøril Torske

behance.net/gtorske

Gøril Torske has worked as a graphic designer for more than 17 years. She holds a bachelor's degree in graphic design from Central St. Martins in London, and a foundation in art history from the University of Bergen, Norway. She is currently working for Mission Design, a studio composed of brand specialists. They work with strategic design to build strong brands for companies, big and small, throughout Norway and Scandinavia.

pp. 82-85

Graphéine

grapheine.com

Graphéine is a graphic design advice agency created in 2002 by like-minded and lively designers from various professional walks of life, all addicted to image. Graphéine is recommended for all projects that involve brand creation, visual identity, publishing, signage, web design, etc.

pp. 20-25, 50-51, 60-67

H3L Studio

h3lweb.com

Hachetresele, AKA H3L, is an independent studio that stands out for innovative ideas and creative work. The team develops commercial and art projects of global significance. Over the past decade, their practice has led to a sustainable approach to architecture, education, and services through a wide range of work. From the beginning of 2004, Hachetresele has participated in many national and international conferences such as MICA BsAs, OFFF Barcelona, DMY Berlin, etc. Hachetresele has been named by the Presidency of Argentina as one of the most relevant studios and recognized as one of the most transcendent creative hubs in Latin America by TASCHEN.

pp. 144-145, 288-289

Happyending Studio

wearehappyending.com

Happyending Studio is a graphic design studio based in Bilbao, Spain, founded in November 2012 by college friends Ángela Alonso and Elena Perea who like working with people. Big or small, they understand projects as collaborations and chances to share the process and get fun. They don't mind design being simple or complex, serious or fun as long as it gives an appropriate answer to a problem.

pp. 252-253

Henrique Dias

behance.net/henrique-dias

A 24-year-old Brazilian designer who loves design. To him, a relevant identity is a powerful tool to increase revenue and strengthen relations with clients. His work focuses on brand services with high quality and transparent processes.

pp. 172-173

Hiromi Maeo - Enhanced Inc.

behance.net/enhanced_hiromimaeo

A Japanese graphic designer with over 20 years' experience who focuses on corporate branding. His design expertise covers a wide range of visual representations for brands. His style is minimalistic and timeless which enhances core essence of the brand. When it comes to CI/VI design, a highly sophisticatedstyle of design process has made his design outstanding. His strengths also include the way he meticulously construct essential shapes on refined grid and his interpretation of the core of the brand.

pp. 88-91, 236-249

Indústria Inc.

industriainc.com.br

Indústria Inc. is a graphic design studio based in São Paulo, Brazil founded in 2015 by two designers interested in bringing new languages to their environment.

pp. 138-139

Jeroen van Eerden

jeroenvaneerden.nl

Jeroen is a 29 years old freelance logo and branding specialist born in Amsterdam, the Netherlands. Currently he's living in Groningen. He has had 6 years' experience in logo and branding design and worked on various projects from all over the globe. He is passionate about all kinds of digital art, branding, print and packaging design, and abstract art. He is always searching for creative and innovative solutions, aiming to reach new and fresh visual results, and getting the best out of each project. His creative artworks have gained him a reputation through publications, features, and interviews.

pp. 122-123

Jon Ander Pazos

jonanderpazos.com

Jon Ander Pazos is an architect and graphic designer from Barakaldo (Biscay) and currently based in Valencia. After fishing his studies in architecture at the School of Architecture of San Sebastián, he moved to Valencia to complete his education with a master degree of multimedia design. He's passionate about graphic arts with a special interest in branding, packaging, motion graphic, and web design. He considers himself as a curious person who loves traveling and learning new things every day.

pp. 234-235

Jorge Castaño
behance.net/jorqe
A freelance graphic and web designer born in Medellín, Colombia.
pp. 42-43

Jurate Gacionyte
jurategacionyte.com
A designer and a student currently in her final year at Central Saint Martins in London, who recently completed an exchange program at School of Visual Arts in New York. Jurate is drawn to bridging different media, seemingly contrasting ideas, and introducing different worlds to each other. She wants to explore the intersections where poetry, philosophy, and science meet design. Jurate is interested in creating well communicated, aesthetically sound, clever, and most importantly, meaningful work.
pp. 110-113

Kalambokis Demetris
behance.net/Demetris_K
Kalambokis graduated in 2000 from a 4-year study program at A.K.T.O. Group (Art & Design School) in Athens as Bachelor of Arts in product design. For almost 15 years he was occupied in working in various architectural and design offices in Athens, specialized in detail design drawing, site-work analysis and time schedules, team coordination, and company guidelines and promotion. Since 2015 he has been working as a freelancer on various graphic design applications including interior design and CAD drafting.
pp. 276-277

Kidstudio
kidstudio.it
An Italian based studio composed of designers growing up in an environment rich in arts and crafts, history and culture.
pp. 26-29

Kovács Levente
leventekovacs.hu/
A graphic designer based in Budapest, Hungary.
pp. 128-129

Kristina Nikaj
behance.net/KristinaNikaj
Kristina Nikaj was born in 1992. In 2012 she enrolled at the NID-new design institute in Perugia, and graduated in design of visual identity systems in 2015.
pp. 220-223

Kuudes Kerros
kuudes.fi
A strategic brand design consultancy founded in 2004. It builds brands that stand out for their customer experience and brand image. The experienced, multidisciplinary team consists of brand strategists, visual designers, architects, interior architects, consumer insight and trend specialists, service designers, packaging designers, copywriters, and digital strategists.
pp. 194-199

La Nacional Estudio Mexicano
lanacionalem.com
A Mexico based agency specialized in branding and packaging.
pp. 76-77

Lee Hyojin
tyo-stitch.com
behance.net/tyodi
Brand experience designer based in Korea who attempts to deliver the differentiated brand experience by boundlessly agonizing at the various intersections of brand and customers. He makes diverse graphic and illustration based attempts, including branding based on both antique and new things, experience and value.
pp. 152-155, 160-163

Lee Wai Lun, Lim Fei Zun, Leong Kah Fai, Foo Chen En

behance.net/wailun826
behance.net/fzlim
behance.net/cofelkf
behance.net/jeun95

Lee Wai Lun, Lim Fei Zun, Leong Kah Fai, and Foo Chen En are aspiring graphic designers from Malaysia.

pp. 118-119

Lucas Gil-Turner

lucasgilturner.com

The team's job is to discover what makes each design unique and promote it so that it is recognizable. They like the strength of a good concept to find consistent and desirable results. They look for different solutions that fit the needs of each project and each client. They believe that a brand that joins strategy and design represents a powerful asset for a company, besides being an effective sales tool and differencing factor from the competition.

pp. 168-171

Lud/co. Studio

estudiolud.co

Lud/co. Studio people are what they do, while what they do is unexpected and exceptional. They set foot into uncharted territory. They are specialized not only in doing what their clients want, but also in doing what is best for them. They make great works from branding to packaging, and from Brazil to the world.

pp. 204-205, 210-211

Maarten Deckers

behance.net/maartendeckers

Maarten Deckers is a Belgium based designer, typographer, and design consultant who creates identities, logos, books, magazines, and all kinds of digital and printed matter for clients and himself.

pp. 100-101

Mads Sæløen

everythingisinteresting.co

Mads Sæløen is a graphic designer currently living and working in Oslo, Norway. He specializes in creating visual identities and editorial design. Mads strives to create interesting and memorable work with the aim of pushing boundaries and challenge the status quo.

pp. 200-201

Maritina Laskaridou

behance.net/laskmari

Maritina Laskaridou is a Greek graphic designer based in Athens and works on a range of projects including art direction, design, illustration, custom typography for the art and design community, music industry, fashion, and more. She loves design and strongly believes that designs that matter have a strong impact to every person's life. With a proven track in advertising in commercial market sector, Maritina Laskaridou gained modern and innovative communication techniques to develop and implement graphic designs.

pp. 150-151

Masaomi Fujita

tegusu.com

A designer born in 1983 in Shizuoka Prefecture, Japan. After graduating from the Faculty of Design of Shizuoka University of Art and Culture, he engaged in planning, editing, and directing for several years. Reinvented himself as a designer, he worked in an advertising production company as a design and art director for cosmetics, fashion, and magazines. He established design office tegusu in 2012 and now performs a wide variety of works from concept planning to CI and VI development for companies and shops including graphic designs and web designs.

pp. 120-121, 132-135, 254-257

MAUD

maud.com.au

Maud creates provocative designs that build brands and businesses. Their approach is honest, driven by human insight and always starts with brand strategy. They're a multi-disciplinary team of thinkers who place function before aesthetic and work to create enduring design solutions that connect with people. They apply design thinking to any shape of problems including brand, environment, communications, retail, motion, digital, and product.

pp. 142-143

Maurizio Pagnozzi

mauriziopagnozzi.com

An Italian designer based in London. He studied graphic design at "Scuolala Tecnica" of Benevento, where he graduated with a project entitled "Anatomy of the typeface." He continued his studies at ILAS of Naples where he studied art direction, copywriting, and graphic design and graduated in 2013 with full marks (110/110 magna cum laude). In January 2014 he returns to Benevento at his old graphics school, but this time as a teacher of visual communication. Teaching supports the freelance activities at his studio One Design. He worked for several international clients which appreciate his direct style, clean and essential, but not devoid of meaning and contents. He specializes in branding, corporate identity, and packaging. His aim is always to create works that combine concepts with strong functional and solid executions.

pp. 202-203, 206-207

Mimética

mimetica.es

A team made up by enthusiasts of creativity, which they interpret as means to generate ideas, a key ingredient in the strategy to find simple, and effective solutions that will create added value for their clients. Starting with a thorough analysis of their clients' needs and incorporating their findings through every stage of the process, they find creative solutions to their problems and create value based on strategy, design, and technology.

pp. 192-193

Mind Design

minddesign.co.uk

Established in 1999, Mind Design is an accomplished design consultancy that specializes in the development of visual identities which include print, web, packaging, and interior graphics. The studio is run by Holger Jacobs who has more than 20 years' experience and worked for a wide range of clients, from start-ups to established international companies. The studio's work has been showcased in various publications.

pp. 30-33, 44-47

Natalia Bivol

nataliabivol.com

An illustrator and graphic designer based in San Francisco, California. She spent her childhood in Moldova, a tiny country in Eastern Europe. Natalia earned her bachelor's degree in Fashion Design in Milan, Italy. Her work is characterized by clean lines and minimal aesthetics. She uses illustration as a visual language and a powerful tool to communicate ideas.

pp. 258-259

Natalia Żerko

behance.net/nataliazerko

Natalia Żerko is a graphic designer and illustrator based in Poznan, Poland. She works independently, but also for Kommunikat —a brand design studio from Poznan, Poland. Aside from branding project for various clients, Natalia's an art director and illustrator. Her work can be seen on multiple design-related websites.

pp. 106-109

Negation Studio
negationstudio.com
Negation Studio, a small graphic design and illustration studio founded by Patryk Hardziej and Patrycja Podkościelny, based in Gdynia, Poland. They Handle projects dealing with illustration, branding, logo design, visual communication, editorial graphics, and art projects.

pp. 140-141

Nephews
losnephews.com
A Mexican design firm dedicated to brand building. The firm is owned by the partners, a group of designers who are leaders in different creative areas. The group includes associated companies and independent artists with the intention to offer their customers everything they need to build their brands. Nephews believes that great design cannot be possible without passion, intelligence, and personal commitment that have been shown in their portfolio of work and over fifteen years' independent professional experience.

pp. 124-125

Nicolas Di Vittorio
behance.net/NicolasDiVittorio
Nicolas Di Vittorio was born on June 30 in 1996 in Bellinzona, a little city of the Italian-speaking region of the Switzerland. He studied Information Technology in Lugano specializing in development. Since his first time using a computer he has always been fascinated by design, so he decided learning new things about it day-by-day by googling anything he was interested in.

pp. 232-233

Nina Gregier
ninagregier.com
Graduated from Academy of Fine Arts in Katowice, Poland, Nina Gregier is now an art director and graphic designer focused on typography, branding, and print design. She is based in Krakow, Poland, but works internationally.

pp. 268-269, 278-279

Nomo® Creative
nomocreative.com
Nomo® Creative is a Taipei-based design studio founded by three designers Yu Chien Lin, Chi Tai Lin, and Chen Huang Chian in 2015. Their services include building brand identity, vectors and fonts creation, bookbinding, showcase visual planning, and packaging design.

pp. 96-99

Ohimena Studio
ohimenastudio.com
Ohimena Studio is a graphic design and visual communication studio based in Milan. It is founded by Luigi Durante and Silvia Pisani with a growing team of creative minds focused on art direction. Ohimena Studio believes that a good visual communication design is mainly based on measuring comprehension by the audience, not on personal aesthetic and/or artistic preference, because there are no universally agreed-upon principles of beauty and ugliness.

pp. 216-219

Olivier Rensonnet
qian.be
A designer who is widely recognized for his love of corporate design, never-ending creative enthusiasm, and the qián agency he founded. He is an identity specialist working with the best professionals in communication for over 15 years. In this period of time, he has managed to develop identities for many companies and institutions, from the smallest to the largest.

pp. 102-103

Oscar Bastidas

mor8graphic.com

Oscar Bastidas Villegas (AKA Mor8) is a 33-year-old Venezuelan art director focused on branding design, with more than 11 years of experience working for international brands like Toyota, Buchanan's, McDonalds, Johnnie Walker, Budget among others, with main beacon on branding and advertising projects. He is developing branding concepts for several companies around the world, like United Estates, Switzerland, Mexico, London, Colombia, and United Arab Emirates.

pp. 148-149

Pablo Chico

behance.net/pchicolin

A graphic designer based in Madrid, Spain.

pp. 280-281

Proxy

proxyventures.com

Proxy is a London-based brand and design studio specialized in building new, global category leading brands, and reimagining existing brands. Proxy's recent work includes brain training brand Peak, wearable brand Ōura and travel brand Faralong.com. Proxy's partners have been responsible for designing the global brand identities for Supercell, Nokia, and Toyota.

pp. 136-137

Rebels Studios

rebelsstudios.com

With the Scandinavian design heritage rooted in its backbone, Rebels Studios add new dimensions to the modernist approach. The team creates brand identities, print materials for ad campaigns, album artworks, package designs, and a whole lot more. When working with traditional media the team always brings a digital perspective by developing strong visual concepts that can live in both worlds.

pp. 250-251

Roger Lara

behance.net/rogerlara

Roger Lara is a professor, strategic design consultant, and the founder of the education platform Brand Inteligente. As a designer, he is enterprising and has more than five years' experience in designing and building brands. He is also qualified in management and strategic design on ITS. He has extensive experience in managing projects from the creation of the proposed strategic value to its full implementation, including the direction and supervision of the project.

pp. 158-159

Studio fnt

studiofnt.com

Studio fnt is a Seoul based graphic design studio that works on prints, identities, interactive and digital media, etc. It collects fragmented and straying thoughts, and then organizes and transforms them into relevant forms.

pp. 228-231

Studio Gris

studio-gris.com

Gris is a creativity studio dedicated to art direction, graphic design, editorial design, illustration, photography, web-design, and well balanced melting pot of these domains. Founded in Paris in 2015 by Marc Azoulay, Jules Pottier and Thomas Romeuf, Gris is animated by the wish of merging these 3 complementary profiles for the creation of an uncluttered, strong, and distinctive design, ensuring to keep the greatest harmony between the picture and the message.

pp. 274-275

Studio Lane

studio-lane.com

Lane is the working practice of graphic designer and creative thinker, Sam Lane. He crafts brand identities, stories, and experiences for a varied list of clients, ranging from international businesses to small start-ups. He is concept driven and believes that every client has an important story that needs to be brought to life in its own unique way. He applies meticulous detail, strategic thinking, skill, and craftsmanship into every stage of his design process, ensuring that he creates honest narratives that are unique and deliver results.

pp. 212-215

Studio Newwork

studionewwork.com

Studio Newwork is a graphic design studio based in New York focusing on branding, editorial, and fashion. It assembles a team of passionate typographic designers with commitment to searching for excellence in design. Studio Newwork designs with passion, care, and love.

pp. 74-75, 270-273

Studio WABA

studiowaba.com

Studio WABA is an independent graphic design studio based in Porto, Portugal, specializing in brand communication, corporate identity, editorial design, exhibition design, and packaging. Its goal is to create honest, intelligent, and timeless work. It takes care of every single step of the graphic design process and collaborates with its clients, big or small, to create thoughtful responses that reflect their needs and values. The team also co-works regularly with architects, interior designers, photographers, web developers, interaction designers, and copywriters to accomplish a full-pack solution for their projects.

pp. 224-225

Supercake

supercake.it

Supercake manages different complex projects at various scales, from the preliminary stage to the executive, working with specialized teams. The design method is intended as a circular process: the sensitivity to the problems and resources (economic, social, and environmental), flexibility of thought, originality, analysis and synthesis, intuition, and redefining.

pp. 18-19

Toormix

toormix.com

Created in 2000 in Barcelona by Ferran Mitjans and Oriol Armengou, Toormix is a mix of a brand consultancy, a design studio and a digital creative agency.

We use strategic thinking and design to create innovative brand experiences across physical, digital or spatial media with a clear focus on user needs, as well as understanding business challenges and objectives.

pp. 12-17

Transform Design

transform.tw

Transform Design is a design studio based in Taiwan. They believe that only through constant change may greater ideas be triggered. Each unique project deserves its own design language, and thus conventional design solutions never meet their high expectations. They set these high standards because they insist that the outcome should be better and more valuable. Their clients come from all industries, ranging from construction, electronics, to fashion, education, and art. They rely on integrative thinking to provide each client of each trade with the most suitable advices and services.

pp. 48-49, 164-167

Weston Doty

westondoty.com

Weston Doty is a New York-based graphic designer and photographer who is passionate about the world of visual communication. He uses multiple skills to create effective

and eye-catching works for brands both big and small.
pp. 146-147

WonderID
wonderid.agency
A logo must be the reflection of a brand's soul and WonderID's mission is to unveil its essence and improve it until they reach the "take your breath away" effect, the same feeling one could get when entering an inspiring and exciting destination. They are branding enthusiasts who deeply believe that their job goes beyond designing a beautiful logo, but is to create new and captivating worlds based on concept and significance.
pp. 130-131

Yorgos Panagopoulos
yorgospanagopoulos.com
Yorgos Panagopoulos is a graphic designer from Athens, Greece. He has a bachelor's degree in graphic design and a master's degree in film directing from the University of Edinburgh. He has designed for a number of clients, from small companies to hospitality chains on a variety of platforms such as print, web, and film. He currently resides and works in the United Kingdom.
pp. 226-227

Zivan Rosic
zivanrosic.com
Zivan Rosic is a Serbian born designer and filmmaker currently residing in Los Angeles. His desired approach to logo and visual identity is always to reduce forms to their most basic essence while still maintaining strong visuals and clear communication.
pp. 208-209

Acknowledgements

We would like to express our gratitude to all of the designers and companies for their generous contribution of images, ideas, and concepts. We are also very grateful to many other people whose names do not appear in the credits but who made specific contributions and provided support. Without them, the successful completion of this book would not be possible. Special thanks to all of the contributors for sharing their innovation and creativity with all of our readers around the world. Our editorial team includes editor Daze Guo and book designer Yunshu Liu, to whom we are truly grateful.